Tara West is the author t
Eaten as a Delicacy in Japan
in Northern Ireland with her husband and
daughter.

Praise for *The Upside of Down*

'Tara West tells the truth - about depression, about writing and about life. Whoever you are, this book will make you feel a lot better.'
Ian Sansom, author of over a dozen books and writer for the Guardian, the Spectator, and the Times Literary Supplement

'I asked myself at every page, can this woman really be depressed if she writes with such energy and candour? But a reader can't doubt experience that is retold so vividly. This is a memoir that opens windows on the soul.'
Malachi O'Doherty, journalist, broadcaster and author

'I loved this book. I felt nostalgia, despair and elation in equal measures and was rooting for the author along the way. The story resonated with my own adolescence touching on growing up, family, love and resilience. An ordinary story in many ways, but told with extraordinary insight and hope.'
Billy Murphy, Director of Mental Health Services, Inspire Wellbeing and Recovery

'*The Upside of Down* is a brilliantly written and engaging memoir, but it offers much more because Tara West shines a light on depression in a way that gives hope to anyone affected by 'mood flu' and I believe this book will help to break the stigma around talking openly about problems with your thinker.'
Tony Macaulay, author of *Paperboy* and peace builder

'Those who still stigmatise mental illness, who insist that depression is something to be dismissed or ashamed of, swept under the proverbial carpet, should be forced to read Tara West's stunning memoir *The Upside of Down* – for it will smash their misguided prejudices to smithereens. Compelling, raw and achingly honest, the memoir is exquisitely written, and punctuated with West's trademark piercing humour. I cried, I laughed, and I marvelled at her resilience, her courage and her authenticity. Tara West is one of our most talented writers who has never quite received the accolades she deserves. *The Upside of Down* will surely right that wrong.'
Lesley Allen, author of *The Lonely Life of Biddy Weir*

The Upside of Down

Tara West

Dalzell Press

First published in 2020 by Dalzell Press

Dalzell Press
54 Abbey Street
Bangor, N. Ireland
BT20 4JB

ISBN 978-1-8380871-0-4

Cover design by Karen Vaughan
Cover image © Catherine MacBride/Stocksy

Supported by the National Lottery though the Arts
Council of Northern Ireland

LOTTERY FUNDED

For Mummy.
In the next room.

Prologue

'Dave,' I say.

We're sitting in our small living room, watching TV, drinking up the last of the weekend. Dave is wearing his favourite red and black striped jumper and he's sprawled across the settee. I'm on the floor, chest pounding.

'Dave.'

'What?'

'I don't feel right.'

'What?'

I cover my face with my hands and stop breathing. I know I'm acting weird, I know I look weird. He's beside me now.

'What's wrong, what is it?'

'I don't feel right.'

'What do you mean?'

How can I tell him? There is no way to say it, but it's too late, I've started and I can't go back.

'What is it, what's wrong?'

I am lost I am lost I am lost.

'Move your hands. What is it? You're scaring me.'

I don't want to tell him. I don't want to say the words that will break everything apart. But I'm lost and I need someone to lead me out of the dark.

I move my hands away from my face. 'I want to kill myself.'

I had a loving husband, a kind mother, a decent family, good friends and a successful career in advertising. My first novel had just been published. What was there to be unhappy about? But I was beyond unhappy. Every day I'd get random glimpses of slicing open my own flesh, like a flashback to something that hadn't happened yet. I could see my skin peeling back like loose sheets of leather, revealing my workings, releasing my guts, opening me up and spilling me out. I wanted to peel myself to death. I couldn't bear myself, inside or out.

I was sick, but it was my brain that was ill – or rather, the bit inside my brain that was me. I had overdosed on brainwaves. I had mood flu. I'd hurt my thinker. I'd been diagnosing and treating my own illnesses since I was seventeen, but this time, no painkiller was going to do the job. I couldn't clean it up, smother it with Savlon and apply a plaster. I didn't know what to do. I'd never been sick like this before and I didn't know anyone who had.

Before

Tara West

Mothers

I was sitting on the end of the bed my mother and I shared. Our room was at the back of our small maisonette, which caught the sun in the evening, but the window was small and the thin slats of the Venetian blinds made the room dim. A bedside lamp cast a gentle light over the flowery bedspread.

My mother sat beside me, smelling of talc and soft things. She was forty-three and I was fourteen. I had hair like Siouxsie Sioux, although today it hung at half-mast.

'What are you crying for?' she said, with kindness.

'Because...' I sucked in a shaky breath. All my punky make-up was gone, wiped over all my sleeves. I wasn't a girl for tissues.

'I'm crying because...' I could barely speak. My grandmother would be buried the next day. 'I'm crying because...' I crumpled up, breathless. '...because you have no mummy.'

It was not my grandmother's death that broke my heart, but the thought of my own mother being motherless. Losing my mother was the worst thing I could imagine; I couldn't bear to think that she was left to cope alone, abandoned, with no one to care for her. But Mummy wasn't crying, and she didn't cry the day of the funeral either.

She sat closer on the bed and took my hand, gliding her thumb back and forth across my fingers.

'Ach Tara,' she said. And that was all.

My mother told me nothing about her relationship with her mother until I was in my twenties, and even then, the words escaped her sporadically and quietly, like a cough that hoped not to be noticed. Over the years, her references and recollections revealed a lonely childhood accompanied by a constant stream of criticism.

'You nearly killed me,' my grandmother told my mother of her breech birth, as though she had done it out of spite. When my mother was pregnant with her second child shortly after her first was born, my grandmother said, 'You're the kind of woman who makes slums.' My own mother had indulged my spark, curiosity and edge, and I was enraged on her behalf. She didn't deserve such treatment, no one did. But her way of coping was to bring up her own children patiently, tenderly and lovingly.

So my experimental hair, outrageous clothes and reading of unsuitable material were tolerated without comment. My enormous soaped-up hair which I hacked at with nail scissors, my PVC mini-skirt, fishnet tights and DM boots were ignored. Mine was a gentle teenage rebellion, and relatively easy to manage. I may have looked startling, but tucked away in our bedroom I enjoyed my homework, read incessantly and wrote novels in secret exercise books. I was easy, as teenagers go.

After my grandfather died, my mother, grandmother and I went on a bus trip to the north coast. Next to me, my mother was the youngest on the bus. The seats were filled with elderly couples, widows, widowers and ancient powdery friends who rocked and cackled together. It was the eighties and everything was brown: beige trousers, camel coats, sandy twinsets, chocolate patent handbags, seats the colour of HP Sauce. The bus was a rainbow of drying mud. My grandmother looked shaken and vulnerable at the stares and double-takes her granddaughter invited, as I boarded the bus draped in chains and studs, my fishnets disappearing into fluorescent green socks. She did not normally do buses. She most certainly did not draw attention to herself. This was unfamiliar territory, used as she was to being ferried everywhere in my grandfather's baked-bean-brown Austin Allegro, with him at her heel wherever they went, boosting her with his hovering support. She did not mix with hoi polloi, even though she was as hoi and polloi as the rest of us.

Her dignity and superiority were important to her, which made me think she was insecure and felt frequently threatened, perhaps because she came from a working-class family that had almost reached middle class. Her own father was a printer and lithographer who loved music and played piano. He and his wife started a family in their thirties, but they died in their early fifties, leaving my grandmother and her four siblings to support themselves from a young age.

My grandmother worked in a mill, then married my grandfather who came from a long line of carters with a stable of Clydesdales at the docks. They moved to a small semi on a wide arterial route out of the city, a step up from the mill-shadowed terraces of north Belfast.

From a young age I've been analysing people, so I can understand their motivations and often excuse them, but my mother never did. All she knew was that she was not good enough for her own mother. Her brother, eleven years her junior, was pampered and admired, while she was disapproved of. I don't have an explanation and neither did she. When criticised, she accepted it and believed it. But when it came to me, her youngest daughter, she took a stand. I was her blonde bright-eyed baby who'd turned into a creative, if rather alarming to look at, teenager, who shared her own sensitivity and absurd sense of humour. She made it clear to my grandmother that my imperfections were normal and that criticism was irrelevant. I was a child, and doing what children do. My mother told my grandmother I would grow out of it. And I did, mostly, but my grandmother died before that happened. It was a quiet victory for my mother, if she'd ever thought about it in those terms, which I'm sure she didn't.

Sindy dies

My mother had four children and I was the 'artistic one', the one who craved and coveted blank paper to write on, paint or cut up. I was tomboyish and hot-tempered, and I liked Tomorrow's World, the Open University and Monty Python, even though I didn't understand half of what was going on. I loved school and was disappointed when I didn't learn to read on my first day. When I did learn, I hoovered up books and grew frustrated at the plodding progress of the classroom. I wasn't dazzlingly clever, nor was I encouraged to study, but I did like learning and I liked to see my name beside a column of gold stars. I liked getting things right.

Dolls and prams horrified me; I preferred to send my much-loved Teddy, inappropriately dressed Ballerina Sindy and my brother's Action Man on perilous adventures below the kitchen table. I took myself and any friend who would come on imaginary troglodytic journeys below the shade of next door's ornamental cherry tree. My sisters were six and seven years older than I was and into the Bay City Rollers. My brother was three years older and interested in running, shouting and kicking a ball. Only rain and captivity made us play together, and by play I mean they played and I whined, endlessly losing out to their big-kid Monopoly and Battleship strategies.

Rathcoole, where we lived, was an estate six miles north of Belfast, built in the fifties and sixties to house families who would otherwise have lived in the crowded and sectarian streets of the city. Our house was in an older part of the estate, where the neighbours were decent and kids were uncomplicated, playing with skipping ropes and bikes. My father was a docker, like his own father and his father too. We had enough money for shoes from Clarks, holidays on the north coast and a roast every weekend. I shared a room with my brother, who hid his packed lunches in a suitcase under his bed because he couldn't bring himself to tell our mother he didn't like Heinz Sandwich Spread. A sentimental bunch, we were, and in our house, safe.

Then the docks changed. Workers were made redundant and my father was one of them. Having begun work at thirteen, delivering bread on a bicycle, all the skills he had were in 'unskilled' work. He was lean, rangy and at six foot four, unusually tall for an Ulsterman. His physical strength and nervous energy landed him a series of temporary labouring jobs, including emptying bins and lifting timber, but when the work ran out, he joined the ranks of the unemployed. With limited schooling, he relied on my mother to fill out forms, write letters, make appointments and deal with officialdom, and the thought of signing on at 'the bru' was worrying for him. His writing was slow and awkward. Knowing that made him anxious, which made things worse. He needed my mother's support.

For the first eight years of my life, I barely remember my mother expressing anything but love, and that was directed at us, her children. I remember her laughing at my father when he put his foot in a bucket of paste when he was redecorating the hall, but I don't remember her laughing with him. They did not kiss, hug or hold hands. They never seemed to have much to say to each other. They married within months of meeting, she having fallen pregnant at the age of nineteen. He was thirty-two, good-looking and strong, and I have no doubt he loved her, but it was an awkward match. He was a labourer with patriarchal leanings, and she was a grammar school girl, bright and well read. She told me later that she often mistook sex for love, and I understood how that might happen. However, fifteen years and four children into the marriage, she had gained perspective.

She was angry that day, I could tell. Unpractised in the expression of anger, it leaked out through her tight lips, stiff shoulders and hard sighs. She was angry because he wouldn't go to 'the bru' to sign on alone, so she had to go with him, which meant I had to go too, and I was sick. We had no car, we had to walk, and I vomited the whole way. It was less than a mile, but to a vomiting eight-year-old, it may as well have been three leagues up a mountain. I waited outside the benefits office, sweating in the cold, and stared at by passers-by as my stomach writhed up my gullet. I was sick, tired and weak, but as long as I had my mother, I could cope. For her though, it was like having five children, not four. If she'd had the words or the confidence, she might have told him to grow up, take it on the chin, and don't force a child onto her feet and across the estate to the benefits office when she's sick and has no business being there in the first place. But she didn't say anything. They filled in the forms and we went home in silence. I think he carried me.

His redundancy payout meant new furniture, Venetian blinds, a SuperSer heater and a new fridge. But by then, there was something different about my mother. She lost weight, experimented with make-up, adjusted her bras to accommodate her slim new figure and bought some sexy high-heeled boots. Suddenly, in her mid-thirties, she was head-turningly foxy. Was it the newfound confidence of realising her own worth, or was it something else? I don't know. All I knew was that one day I had been squeezed into the back seat of my grandfather's Austin Allegro – the first one, the mustard yellow one – between my noisy sisters and brother, being taken to live at my grandmother's house.

'When's Daddy coming?' I asked as we drove. My grandmother sat in front. My siblings stopped talking. My grandfather puffed on his Park Drive. The windows were up. It was the 1970s.

'When's Daddy coming?' I asked again.

My words hung between us like a curtain. Then the conversation resumed. I never got an answer. No one said he wouldn't be coming, no one told me she'd left him. I worked it out from the fact that we were sleeping on the floor of my grandmother's sitting room under her fish-eye mirror and I didn't see my father for months.

Half of our toys were lost in the move, including Teddy, Ballerina Sindy and Monopoly. I imagined Teddy missed me. In my mind he was lying at the dump, lost and alone. My grandmother bought me a new bear for my ninth birthday and we called him Ted, but he was golden and clean, perfectly formed and jointed with a prim pink bow and I worried I would ruin him. I didn't send him on adventures; I left him on my pillow to observe.

Sindy turned up in a plastic bag, along with some plates, a tea towel and a handful of spoons. I dangled her out my bedroom window with a string tied round her neck, making her dance in the overgrown garden of our new house – a maisonette in the newer part of the estate. I believe Sindy was hanged.

Everything changed when my parents separated, including me.

Mad

'I think you should go to work,' Dave says.

We've been up most of the night. My revelation has shocked him. We've been clinging to one another for hours, holding hands when moving upstairs, as though we might be cast away if the link between us is broken. We sleep pressed together like twins and when he gets up in the morning, he sits on the bed, staring at me. I know he doesn't want to go to work. I tell him he should go, that I feel better now, that I'll be OK.

'Phone me?' he says.

'I will.'

'You'll definitely go to work?'

I am in a black tube that runs in every direction. 'Yes.'

'Promise me you'll go.' Maybe he thinks work will protect me while he's not there. 'Promise me you'll phone the doctor.'

I promise. He hugs me for a long time and I smile and tell him not to worry, that I'll phone the doctor. He leaves, and with a huge effort, I sit up and wave out the bedroom window as he drives away. The look on his face makes me wish I hadn't told him. Telling the people closest to you is the best and worst thing you can do.

I have the strangest feeling when I get out of bed, as though my neck is stretched long and snaky like Alice in Wonderland. My soul, or my spirit, or something inside, has collapsed; my mind is concave. I'm too heavy for my own legs, which shake and threaten to drop me. I lean on the wall on my way to the bathroom. My mother always jokingly said, 'Why stand when you can sit? Why sit when you can lie down?' And then she would lie down, fluffy mule slippers aloft.

But I can't sit and I can't lie down, much as my body wants to. I have to go to work, Dave wants me to go, I'm expected to go, I'm never off. I can't phone in sick, I don't know how. What would I say? 'I want to die. It's just a bug. I'll be back tomorrow.'

Work has been a performance for months. There is 'showtime' Tara: happy, energetic, confident, in control, coming up with ideas for ads, presenting to clients, writing scripts. And there is the real Tara: shaking, overwhelmed, lost and empty, wondering how and when the end will come, because come it must. The distance between the two has grown so great, it's become unsustainable. But none of that can be explained in a phone call. I bathe, eat cereal, drink tea, get into my car and drive.

I am convinced everyone else can see me. In their cars, vans, buses and lorries, they all see me. They know, they must know. That blonde who was on the news and in the paper, talking about her book. That's her – look. She's mental. Look at her face, it's shifting and melting, sometimes her head fills the whole car, other times she shrinks to the thinness of paper. She's making noises no one can hear. She's held together with string.

There is something wrong with the world, there's something wrong with my world. I'm fighting a black cloud I can't get hold of. It's crushing me. Look at the people driving to work – they're all OK. Look how OK they are. They're handling life, they're normal and balanced and in control and none of them have fucked things up like I have, like I do. Look at them looking at me, not looking at me. I drive. I'm driving.

I am going mad.

The jungle

'Ah, look, the wee baby is going to bed!'

Hilda Wanky (not her real name) had spied me spying her and she squawked my secret to the whole of East Way. She was right, I was going to bed. I didn't even have the excuse that my mother had sent me to bed. I was ten and I was going to bed because I was tired and I thought I'd read for a bit. Hilda and the other girls were still playing as I closed the curtains. Going to bed at a normal hour was incomprehensible to people like her; she had no normal. To Hilda, I was an oddball: 'not right in the head'. I did things she didn't understand, like reading and skipping and sleeping, and she derided my every move. She and the other girls sported fashionable clothes and they ran fast and feral. I was tubby, pubescent and awkward, and wore tops knitted by my mother. And my mother was not a good knitter.

East Way, on the other side of the estate, was another world. It was dark here, dangerous, and everything I'd learned in my previous life would prove itself worthless. They had different rules. You couldn't say what you thought. No one meant what they said. They spoke fast and sharp. Everyone kept a mongrel and every five paces you would step in a turd. People were furious all the time and every sentence contained at least one bastard, three fucks and a cunt. I learned a whole new vocabulary: fuck, fucken, wanker, fanny, fruit, bollicks, randy, dickhead, hun, headbin, head the ball, lezzer, looper, tits, Tennents, taig, twat and cunt. I asked my brother to say 'H' to find out if he was a Catholic. He laughed his tits off. I learned quickly.

The first time my mother took me to see our new maisonette, she showed me my books, arranged neatly in the corner of the living room – I assume to make it look welcoming. She didn't need to. I was naïve enough not to be afraid. How was I to know we were moving to a jungle? Hilda, Sammy, Wee William, Wee Ray, the kids in East Way were ferocious. Their shared language was malice and I had never learned it. Even their dogs knew it – they swanned and skittered about, sniffing your crotch and baring their teeth to remind you of your place. Our own dog, a soft round Golden Retriever called Bess, was out of her depth. If the other dogs weren't trying to kill her, they were trying to impregnate her. She became an overweight housedog and a footrest for the family, venturing no further than the back garden to do her business. The garden was literally a shit heap.

The back garden had started life as a patch of grass beside a strip of cement, but with neither man nor mower to control the grass or lift the crap, our garden grew into a tall, waving wilderness. The grass and weeds were so long, you could barely see the teabags flicked over the fence by Big Ray, Wee Ray's dad. I have no idea why Big Ray flicked teabags into our garden. Perhaps he felt they would help. Or perhaps he felt oddly threatened by the intelligent and good-looking Joan and her four well-spoken kids and it made him feel better to play tricks on her. Or perhaps he was a sociopath. I don't know.

Granny still took us to church on Sunday, I still played recorder and met with members of the 'Butterfly Club' at school (we made badges with butterflies on), and I never learned the Protestant anthem *The Sash*. I was not born to East Way, I moved there, and it was too late for me. The first nine years of my life had turned me into a pleasant, well-meaning kid and there was nothing East Way could do about it.

Unanswered question

'What's suicide?' I asked my mother.

I thought I had played this one well. I knew that if I asked my mother too soon after my father's visit, when he had pleaded with her at the back door of the maisonette and she had screamed at him to leave, she'd know I'd heard everything they said. So I waited a few days. She'd have forgotten their conversation by then. She wouldn't know I had heard the whole thing.

But I was snared.

She took my hand. 'Where did you hear that word?'

'I just heard it... on TV.'

And now I knew that she knew that I had heard the hysterical argument at the door. I didn't want her to know that I'd heard her sobbing, seen her run up the stairs wailing, watched my sisters tell my father to go away, stared at him as he pleaded and shook his head and caught his tears with two hands at the back door. In some way, I knew I shouldn't have witnessed all this. Somehow, I felt it was my fault that I had.

My mother pulled me close. I don't remember what we talked about, but I know it wasn't the definition of suicide.

Falling out of love

My mother started to snap and shout, and was angry for no reason. She stopped doing housework and made us chips every night, shaking the chip pan roughly and dumping the food onto plates along with buttered bread, as if she hated the cooker, the cooking, the cooked and cooked for. She worked a series of part-time jobs – first, cleaning, which she hated, then bar work, which she seemed to like, but had to stop because someone told 'the bru' she was 'doing the double'.

My clothes wore out and weren't replaced. Everything was getting shorter and tighter, but no new clothes appeared. The old clothes got dirtier and weren't washed. Each day, I selected my clothes from a murky pile on the floor at the bottom of the bed. No one told me to wash myself. I stopped brushing my teeth because no one nagged me to do it. My father had a new job labouring in a bakery, but none of his money went to support us.

My mother hated us, I was sure. She rowed with my sisters, even hitting them once, and my brother stayed away from the house. My newly pubescent body revolted her – surely that was why she didn't cuddle me and disapproved so vocally when I was ill or, as I did just once, wet the bed. My growing body was disgusting to her. I was disgusting. She couldn't bear to have me around. When I was alone, I held her woolly waistcoat to my face, breathing in her smell. I put it back in the same place to make sure no one knew.

She still put on her make-up, dyed her hair and wore her trousers tucked into her high-heeled boots, despite the dire lack of money and her grim mood. The night of Big Belle's clothes party, she looked aloof and in control. Big Belle lived a few doors down and was showing off the new children's clothing range from Freeman's Catalogue. Whoever kept the catalogue wielded the power in the street, and Belle had all the women at her bidding, including my mother. Our coats, plates and bed linen were all from Belle's catalogue, to be paid for over a million weeks. Joan might look lovely, Joan might be educated, but Joan was as skint as everyone else. More so, because she didn't get the commission Belle got.

I remember how I was called in from the street. Inside Belle's house, the living room was foggy with smoke and the walls were lined with chairs on which women pawed over packets of children's clothes. My mother wanted me to try something on, but I knew it was a bad idea. I mumbled and squirmed and the women turned to watch.

'But Mummy...'

'Try it on, love,' Big Belle said. Her huge arms spilled out of her sleeveless smock dress like pitted cones, tapering into short podgy fingers. 'It'll be lovely on you.'

The women clucked and agreed. I moved away, but my mother caught my arm.

'Come on, Tara,' she said in a strange, theatrical voice. She was the centre of attention now and she couldn't let go. That would look like she had no control over her own children. That would make her look stupid and would embarrass her. But if I stayed, I would embarrass her more.

'Mummy...'

She wanted me to take off my T-shirt, but I wasn't wearing a T-shirt – I was wearing a faded yellow vest with nothing underneath, and if I took it off, they would all see my pubescent breasts. Surely she knew that – she could see for herself. But she couldn't stop now; they were all watching.

My mother pulled off what she thought was my T-shirt and I stood there, topless, as they all looked on, smiling awkwardly.

'Where's your ... vest?' my mother laughed in that theatrical voice, pulling a flowery tunic-style dress over my head.

She turned me this way and that, pretending to check the fit of the dress. It was, of course, too small and the flowery pattern totally unsuitable. I couldn't wear children's clothes anymore. I needed women's clothes, and very soon, tomorrow even, I would need a bra. She pulled off the dress, I put on my faded yellow top and left, sweating and red-faced.

Later, at home, she was tight-lipped. 'I was so embarrassed tonight,' she said. 'Why did you have no vest on?'

I wanted to say to her that I only have one vest and I'm wearing it because I don't have any clean T-shirts and I don't ask for new clothes or clean clothes because you might shout at me, and anyway, why should I ask for clothes when you're my mummy and you're supposed to get me vests and T-shirts like the other mummies do? If any of the other mummies had called their kids in from the street, their kids would have had T-shirts *and* vests on, so this isn't my fault, it can't be and it isn't. Even though I was young, I had observed and understood the dynamics, I understood about humiliation and saving face, but I couldn't articulate any of it. So I said nothing. I didn't want her to feel blame. I stood there, reddening, looking stupid.

I stopped asking for anything, or making demands for attention, or admitting I was ill or sad or hungry – risking any kind of disapproval. I watched TV, disappeared into books, did my homework and read my mother's mind constantly, believing she thought I was disgusting and stupid. I developed a rash across my toes so painful I could barely walk, and I had a cold that lasted a year. I cried on the way to school and wiped it away before I arrived. The soles on my shoes flapped like long dog tongues and a man tried to feel me up in a subway. But I said nothing.

I felt nothing when she asked if I would like to spend six weeks with a family in America. That was fine. They would find me disgusting too.

She couldn't know I was depressed; her anger, distance and neglect were out of character, it was likely she was depressed too. But mental illness wasn't discussed then – it was unmentionable, to be feared and avoided, if it was even recognised – which meant there was no one to support her, or her children. Perhaps she feared, as I did years later, that if she admitted how desperate she was feeling, her children would be taken away from her.

After America, things changed again.

Ea ea ea ea...

In the ad agency, my desk is made of pale green glass, and on it sit my Mac, a sleek silver lamp and some well-thumbed books. My chair – expensive, soft, leather – sits beside French doors which open onto a small plant-lined, pink-pebbled yard. The office I share with my boss is tasteful and it's making me sick. Maybe it isn't. Something's making me sick. I don't know what it is, but I know I am not well. My heart has expanded to fill the top half of my body, the muscle so huge it's choking me. My fingertips leave crescents of sweat on the green glass. I wipe my hands on my clothes. I can't stay here. I will faint, or shriek, or die. I smooth my hand across my forehead. My mother used to do that to me when I was little.

I perch on my chair and open my email. Clicking and clicking, doing work. Anything from my publisher. No. Fuck's sake. But then again, thank God. I can't do any more for them. Why don't they email me? Here's her email. *Ea, ea, ea, ea*. They hate me. I can't type, I can't think, there is static and snow where my thoughts used to be. Ideas and scripts and presentations and readings. I click on the receive button and the Mac makes a blank sound. I want to go home. What kind of sick is this, how to tell my boss, what do I say? I have a cold. My cold hasn't cleared up. Oh, OK, she says. Hope you feel better soon. What the fuck am I doing smiling at her? Inside my head there is gum stretched in fifty different directions. It will snap, there will be nothing.

I leave the office, but my feet are slabs and they drag along the pavement. There are letters in my head and I can't get them out *ea ea ea ea*. I'm light, lighter than ever. I'm so light in my car as I drive and the sun is out and I'm driving through the city centre and I'm going home with *ea ea ea* I am transparent I'm a sliver I have disappeared.

In bed. In my clothes in my bed in the morning. Don't phone me Dave, please don't phone, and he phones and I can't lie to him. I am lost I am lost I am lost.

I am having a breakdown. Dave makes an appointment for me with the doctor, but it's a week away.

There is immediate help available, and we need it, but we don't know about it. How could we? This has never happened to us before, no one has ever talked to us about it, there have been no ad campaigns on TV saying what to do when you've lost your mind. You can call the Samaritans when you want to kill yourself, but this feels different. I'm not standing with a gun to my temple. Everything inside me has crashed. I've gone mad, I'm not right in the head. I don't think they deal with that, do they? (Turns out they do. They deal with any kind of mental crisis.)

We don't consider a doctor. GP Out of Hours service is available for urgent care, but we don't know that. A good GP could provide an explanation, advice, a reassuring safe haven, if even just for a short while. It's classic burnout, they might say. A breakdown. It happens. Don't panic. But we have no idea. We know nothing about mental illness and we don't recognise it. We cower in bed, eyes open, terrified of what is happening, of what we don't understand. Dave thinks I should phone my mum. I say no, it will only worry her. I say I'll be OK. I'll be OK. We are cast into the dark together.

What I learn in the land of dishwashers

Will and Julia Van Dale, of Susanville, California, were the parents of a little girl called Jodi, but for six weeks during the summer of 1982, they took in two more girls – 'disadvantaged' children from the 'war-torn' streets of Belfast. The Van Dales were supporting one of many charitable schemes created by philanthropists and paid for by donations and host families, whose aim was to bring together children from both sides of the community and allow them to experience a country where everyone had a distinct cultural identity and where everyone still got along,

It was an admirable endeavour and it was lost on me. I didn't know anything about my Protestant 'heritage' - my parents never thought it worth sharing and I didn't study it at school. I did learn about Viking invasions though. I didn't have any issues with Catholics, or with Vikings. My sister had a Catholic boyfriend and a few years later they got married. I had Catholic cousins and I saw similarities between their church and the Church of Ireland we went to. I went on to marry a man who looked like a Viking. Years later, I asked my mother why she felt I should go on a trip that was supposed to change my bigoted ways. She said it was an opportunity to be enlightened in other ways, one she couldn't provide herself.

Children were selected through churches and schools, and an inoffensive boy from my primary school called Ian, and I, were sent off to

35

America to renounce our intolerant ways. Ian went to the east coast and I went to the west, paired off with a girl called Pauline from west Belfast. Pauline was four months older than me, but hadn't hit puberty yet. She was tiny, blonde and cute, and keen to be American. Within days she had an accent and was complaining to Julia, in her twangy new voice, that I had called her a twerp.

Kind, patient, liberal Julia took me into a bedroom and we had a serious talk. About twerps. She thought I was bullying Pauline because I was a Protestant and Protestants were known to persecute Catholics. She said she didn't know what a twerp was. Did Protestants call Catholics twerps in Ireland? I began to explain that Pauline wanted to sit and talk about the boys across the street rather than race up and down on bicycles and a twerp was... well, a twerp was... I began to doubt myself. Maybe twerp... was another way of saying twat. Had I called Pauline a twat? Maybe I was bigoted and didn't know. Oh no! I saw the shift in Julia's eyes – she had witnessed the conflict first-hand and had helped a young Protestant see the error of her ways.

It was not my intention to call Pauline a twat; I was just a girl who wanted to ride bikes and had no interest in boys. Even my mother said twerp. Jeepers, if only Mummy knew. But I said nothing. I couldn't articulate my understanding of Julia's assumptions or define my objections or point out that this was a storm in a teacup, not a symptom of deep-seated intolerance. I was already willing to let others be right and take the blame for being wrong.

Julia didn't appear to find me stupid or disgusting though, despite my terrible blunder. She wasn't angry or reproving, she was optimistic. I might be a bully and a bigot, but she would help me. She would work with me so that I would become more accepting of Pauline, and thereby the whole Catholic population of Ireland, and probably everyone in the world. She was kind and responsible, if a little misguided, and we would all move on, kindly and responsibly. She said I should say sorry to Pauline, and I said I would, although I wasn't entirely convinced twerp was such an awful word. It felt unjust, but I apologised anyway.

Twerp-gate aside, Pauline and I bonded over the neighbours' boys' names, Tracy (a girl's name where we came from) and Randy (to us, a word meaning horny). But over the course of the six weeks I grew closer to Julia, rather than Pauline. Pauline and Jodi became BFFs. They shared the same bedroom, wore each other's clothes and talked about what fucking meant. Julia gave me some second-hand clothes donated by her friend and took me to Walmart to get a bra and some Ban antiperspirant. She introduced me to Kool-Aid, Big Red gum and Oscar Mayer Weiners, and fed me spaghetti Bolognese, salt popcorn, salami sandwiches and home-made waffles soggy with maple syrup. She was an excellent cook, but she also encouraged us to get outside and burn it off. And because it rarely rained, we spent every day in the California sunshine. Rather than learning to live a less bigoted life, I learned what it was like to live a normal eleven-year old's life.

The Van Dales were not overly wealthy by American standards, but they did have three bathrooms, air con, a double garage, two cars, two freezers, a caravan (with a freezer), two dogs, two previous marriages, a dishwasher, a basement, a tree house and countless fragrant pine trees in their garden. At the end of the summer I went home a stone lighter, tanned from head to toe, with a new understanding of the world I lived in. The maisonettes were full of complete and utter headbins, I clearly didn't belong there, and I needed to get out. I needed to make stackloads of money and get a big house with a dishwasher like the Van Dales. Nothing had changed as far as Catholics were concerned. I still liked them, even those who occasionally descended into twerpdom. Most of all, I wanted a good dictionary for Christmas.

Teenage wasteland

At the end of my summer in California, I moved up to an all-girls grammar in the genteel coastal town of Whitehead, about twelve miles from Rathcoole. It was a long daily bus ride there and back, and I started early and returned home late. I spent my evenings in my bedroom studying, drawing, writing and listening to the radio. Songs about tragedy and self-destruction were my favourite. I could even play the theme tune to M.A.S.H. on the recorder. I worked my way through the list of books the 'A' Level girls were required to read and no longer mixed with the kids of East Way; what with the commute, the homework, The Smiths, Charles Bukowski, Charles Dickens and Oscar Wilde, I rarely saw any of them.

'Isn't this a bit grown up for you?' my mother asked, leafing through the jumbo collection of works by Oscar Wilde I'd brought home from the library. She was back to herself again – warm, funny and affectionate. She hugged and kissed me and told me she loved me every day before I left for school. And yet. Walking to the bus stop, listening to seagulls whirling and wheeling above, sitting on the steamy bus with schoolmates in their uniforms, legwarmers and Sony Walkmans, there was always something in the way. A weight, a low note, that stayed with me wherever I went. I knew I was loved, but there was something. Just something.

I listened to my classmates' stories of camping in France and jaunts to London, and their fantasies about sporting heroes and pop stars, and I acted like it was my life too. But I wasn't like them. I didn't explain how I'd just been on a holiday for 'disadvantaged' kids or how I usually spent my holidays in the chair nearest the TV. I never mentioned how I'd lived in the years preceding high school, or the poverty we were still scraping through, or that I saw the lost old people, dirty children and shoplifting drunks they didn't see. These girls led nice lives. Let them enjoy them.

The local education board provided free meals for children of families in receipt of benefits, so I was guaranteed at least one meal of greenish potato and pie a day. I hoped for the best, but suspected the worst of everyone, and I was worried the girls at school would mock me for receiving 'free dinners'. But no one even mentioned it. I was surprised and relieved. Every day lots of girls, in receipt of free *and* paid for meals, queued at a hatch in the wall of the music room, which doubled as the dinner hall. Here, girls were allowed to put posters on the walls and Boy George rubbed shoulders with Bauhaus, Kajagoogoo, Prince and The Smiths.

In this room, with its smoky old piano, parquet floor, cracked windows and pop heroes, I met girls with stories that followed them like spotlights: Aideen the vegetarian Buddhist punk, Daniella the anorexic, Tina who wore dark glasses all day, and Shelley who fizzed with energy and was later expelled for being marvellously mad and uncontrollable. Legendary girls whose wavelength I recognised, but unlike them, I had no legend and no story to tell. I was devastatingly poor, had bad teeth and skin, liked writing and drawing, and... The End.

These girls were creative, bright and talented; they were admired and respected by pupils and often indulged by teachers. They looked different too – they did interesting, often ugly things with their hair, make-up and uniform. They had intelligent expressions and thoughtful voices. And what I liked best about them – they didn't ridicule or laugh at people like me. They talked to everyone. They didn't view themselves as superior, even though I felt they had every right to. They weren't a 'gang'. They just sat together occasionally at lunchtime and anyone could stop by for a chat – the good, the bad and the ugly. Seized by awe and an acute awareness of my inferiority, I clammed up in their presence, laughing in the right places, but eating fast and getting out. Oblivious to my discomfort, they insisted on chatting anyway.

Inspired by the girls' experimental looks, I morphed into a new version of me, first channelling a fair-haired Siouxsie Sioux, then discovering my own quirky brand of punk: my brother's old black shirt, a butchered mini kilt, some fluorescent accessories, and gold and red spiked hair. I would have given anything to own a pair of bondage trousers, they were just so... bondagey, and they were available to order from the back pages of Melody Maker. But the punks in London seemed to have much more money than I did, so I would just have to be creative. I took a pair of trousers donated by my sister, threw them in the bath, splattered them with bleach, then sprayed them with gold car paint and scribbled on them with a marker. They looked amazing and lasted two weeks.

If you're going to avoid the whole issue of not having the money to be fashionable, being original and creative is a good opt-out. 'Oh, I'm much too individual to wear legwarmers and ra-ra skirts and fingerless gloves, you know.' I was not a sheep, I was a peacock. I was not poor, I was making a statement. I invited sniggers and comments wherever I went, and the kids of East Way stared at me slack-jawed. At last, I had confounded them! Huzzah! But best not to say huzzah in front of them for fear of physical attack. (It was a very good dictionary, by the way. I spent a lot of time reading it.)

Most of the time they left me alone, but there were moments when they still let me know my place. Sneers and jeers were fine, stone-throwing and flying kicks I didn't much like.

Invisible friends

When my grandmother died, my mother used some of the money she inherited to have a smart picket fence built round our front garden. It was a pretty thing, ill-at-ease in the neglected quarters of East Way and built close to the site of the annual twelfth of July bonfire. Whether my mother recognised it as such, it was a clear marking out of territory. Joan had fenced the neighbours off. She might chat with them at the shops or order from Belle's catalogue, but she was not one of them.

I had other 'friends' now anyway, I didn't need the kids of East Way – some were at school, and some were imaginary ones I wrote stories about on my way home on the bus: Foxy, Mandy, Minto and Fitzy, punks who played in a band and were very nice to each other, because I couldn't bear to introduce conflict.

I would follow the mundane adventures of Fitzy after I finished my homework or at weekends when I had nothing else to do. When I ran out of ideas for Fitzy the punk, I would follow the adventures of Fitzy the wild child, who had floppy blonde hair and lived in America, abandoned by his parents and living outside the law.

Another story I pursued was a dystopian fantasy about teenagers fighting shadowy government forces, with a long-haired Fitzy who could heal people and who collapsed regularly, poor thing. Books and writing meant I always had somewhere to go, either a world created by me or someone else. Between that and watching TV, it was barely noticeable that I had no life.

My mother tried to encourage me to strike up a friendship with the daughter of the new next-door neighbour. She was the same age as me, orange-skinned and her hair was felt-tip yellow. She was pregnant within months of moving in, whereupon she was taken on a whirlwind tour of all that's good in life – Disneyland Paris, the Top of the Pops studios, Madame Tussauds – before her baby came along and presumably life stopped. I still had no interest in boys. Well, that's not strictly true. I had an interest in boys who were androgynous, gay or dead. I also liked girls who were androgynous, gay or dead.

I remember sitting in my bedroom crying over my confusion. I didn't want to be a lesbian. I didn't want a boyfriend either. I would have made a good fag hag, and I did have one gay friend, but his fag hag was Aideen the vegetarian Buddhist punk, and they volunteered together at Oxfam. It was Aideen who fixed me up with my first 'boyfriend' – Billy. We broke up after three weeks. He was a great guy, with his magic mushroom habit, love of Bob Dylan and anarchy tattoo on his forehead, but I wasn't ready for a relationship. Snogging and sitting was actually pretty tedious.

Gothic love

I spent Saturday afternoons with a few girls from school, hovering round the periphery of young punks and goths who gathered in the centre of Belfast. We were never confident enough to join them, so we stood nearby and practised looking cool/aloof/tortured. We stole nail polish and pens from department stores, and paid good money in bookshops, record shops and Topshop.

It was outside Topshop that I first saw Michael Murphy. Oh Michael. You beautiful thing, with your green eyes, olive skin, spiky black hair and black bondage trousers, and your gorgeous girlfriend Emer, who looked exactly like you, only smaller, and with slightly less make up. How I loved you both, but you especially, and then I knew, at last and for sure, that it was boys more than girls.

I was back to my chubby old self by then, my DIY style was more weird than punk and my asymmetrical long-short bleached hair was just bizarre. You never noticed me, Michael. In the presence of such physical beauty, I melted further into the shadows. I was brutally ugly, I knew, and henceforth I wasn't even going to try. Except for the time I brought my second-hand acoustic guitar into town just so I could impress you by carrying it, Michael, and you might think I was like, you know, Suzanne Vega or something. You didn't notice me that day either. I later learned that you were very short-sighted and too vain to wear your glasses.

Believing I was ugly as well as disgusting, I made no efforts where boys were concerned. I ignored them completely and disappeared into my studies and my writing. My old friend Cheryl, who I'd known since Primary One, told me that I was going to be a writer. It was what I spent all my free time doing; that, and sending longhand manuscripts to publishers, who kindly returned them intact and unread, and while I felt she was right, my mind was set on Art College. I had always been good at art, other people said I was good, and when I wrote about art and artists, I got A's and A+'s. No one said I was good at writing. I fancied myself a fine artist, although that might mean living in poverty, so maybe I'd be a graphic designer instead. There was plenty of money in that. Probably.

I thought Art College was where I belonged. I was wrong.

Drowning

We sat in the dingy, claustrophobic café in the old Co-op building across the road from the Art College drinking watery cappuccino. My mother and I often met for a coffee and a caramel square in town, when we'd huddle close and she would tell me about the kind of life she imagined I would have – the large double-fronted house, the beautiful children, the pots of money; fantasy sessions that probably had the same effect monkeys get from grooming one another. She refreshed and distracted me, and I suspect I did the same for her. I still didn't ask her for things, but she bought me little gifts anyway: books of poetry, an LP or cassette, a magazine or chocolate.

I'd received a grant to study on the Foundation Course at Ulster University Belfast, still known as the Art College, and the course would take a year to complete. After that I would apply to do a degree in design or fine art or textiles. I was the first of our family to go on to third level education and this was a big deal. Things started going wrong before the first term began. My portfolio was good, and I was accepted onto the course before I sat my 'A' Level exams, but that wasn't why I stopped caring. I ran out of energy. I'd learned enough over the years to earn decent marks in the exams, but I had lost interest. I walked out of exams early, writing enough to get me a decent grade and no more. I stopped writing and drawing. I stopped reading. I watched TV blindly, lying on the settee. I had a head made of fudge.

My mother and I had moved from East Way to a sixth floor flat in one of Rathcoole's four tower blocks. My sisters and brother had jobs, partners and were starting families, and my mother had a new partner herself, spending weekdays at his house and staying in the flat with me at weekends. Most nights I had dinner with them, then walked home and buzzed her with two rings on the phone when I was safely in. Her new partner wouldn't have been my choice for her; he had been interned in the 1970s and was now in local politics, ran a mobile shop and drove the biggest car in the street. He probably had as many enemies as he had admirers and I think he saw her as a trophy. I assume my mother was flattered he chose her.

I made my own breakfast and lunch, washed my own clothes, went to bed at a decent hour, then got myself up and out to school in the morning. I didn't always make it there. Often, I would stay on the bus and do the round trip home again, asking my mother to phone the school to say I was sick. I probably was.

I carried an enormous portfolio on the bus every day and I was eccentric and solitary, but I was utterly sane compared to some of the people in the flats: I heard domestic abuse in the flat above, the man next door to me had no nose (there were teeth marks where it been bitten off), the neighbour across the hall polished the lift doors with baby oil, below me lived a paramilitary who was bullied by his wife, there were gunshots on the stairwell, someone took a dump in the communal hallway and some other charmer threw cabbages from the 14th floor.

Maybe it was me. Maybe I attracted completely crazy people. I was a magnet for mental cases. Or maybe the world was full of mental people and in flats they were more noticeable for their saturation. Maybe it was just Rathcoole. Or more likely, I only saw the negatives and was blinkered to the good people and good things. I was more determined than ever to get out, gritting my teeth when I thought of all the places I could go, the success I would be. And suddenly, I wasn't going anywhere. I wasn't even treading water. I had just stopped.

In the café, my mother handed me a little teddy bear and said, 'Here you are. That's to cheer you up.'

I started to cry. She could have given me a squeaky banana or a novelty dancing penis, it wouldn't have mattered, anything and everything was going to make me cry. I wasn't well. But I didn't know. I thought I was stupid and talentless – that's why I was fucking up my first year at Art College. I couldn't manage the projects, I squirmed at the thought of attending the classes and I was sure the lecturers were looking at me funny. They wondered what I was doing there and how I managed to be accepted in the first place.

She held my hand and ran her thumb over my fingers.

Your art is wrong

My first lecturer, let's call him John Dickhead, was a short Englishman who walked in long strides, turned in sudden pirouettes, and wore denim top and bottom. He tucked his chin into his fist as he considered our life drawings, rolling his eyes and making faces at our work. For me, drawing was a release. I was a good draughtsman and I disappeared into a zone when I drew. It felt good and the results were good, I could see it myself. John hooted that I had drawn the model's chair like a child. I had coloured it in. It was silly and ridiculous.

I suppose if I hadn't been feeling so wobbly, I could have accepted his criticism, fixed that part of the drawing, and moved on. I could have seen the reality – that he was a fussy old fart who dyed his hair, who liked to make students feel small so he could feel big, and who was counting the days till his retirement in a grim little fug of frustration and self-hatred. But I froze. He was right. It was crap. It was almost perfect and then I completely fucked it up. Idiot. What a mess. I was crap.

A few weeks later, he wanted to see my ideas book, which should have been brimming with clever thoughts but was, in fact, empty. With a look of contempt, he asked why. I shrugged. He thought I was vacuous, a waste of space. I hadn't an idea in my frothy blonde head. He was right. I was empty. I had no ideas. There was nothing inside, not even language. I avoided him and spent my time in the bar with bohemian Aoife and a beat poet lookalike called Frank, who talked easily of their huge families in the country and made me laugh. Through them I met Eddie, Pete, Bronagh, Ian, Diljit and Matt. Over the course of the year I went out with Matt and Eddie, but the relationships only lasted a few weeks. I couldn't let my guard down; they would only be disappointed and/or disgusted when they got to know me.

I began to draw images of a body drifting under black water, sometimes close up where I could see the blank face, and sometimes in the distance, where the body was almost enveloped by the dark. It was what I saw when I tried to think. I produced the image over and over. I didn't know what it meant, it wasn't an idea, it didn't become anything, it didn't change or grow. The body floated and drifted, helpless and lifeless, and yet somehow still alive. I produced the images mechanically, churning them out in black crayon, knowing I couldn't submit them for any of the units I was studying.

Aoife and Frank were making plans for the summer. They and a bunch of friends were going to rent a house in Donegal, did I want to come? I said I was broke, I needed to work, I would see them in the autumn when we came back to start our degrees.

But I wouldn't see them. I missed my interview for the degree course. I got the date wrong and hadn't the energy to try to set up something new. They wouldn't want me there anyway. I was stupid to think I could succeed. I was out of the Art College with nothing planned.

I developed a rash over my arms and legs and pains in my joints. I did little during the day, I was exhausted, my feet were dead weights and the doctor could find nothing wrong. He suggested some kind of virus. Neither he nor I had any idea what was going on. All I knew was that I had fucked up Art College from start to finish, I'd disappointed my mother – her dreams of my escape, my success, my new life, were over – and it was too much effort to start planning afresh. I stopped drawing, stopped everything, and stayed in the flat. It became a burrow and I went into hibernation.

Dr Pooh-Pooh

After my breakdown, I take three days off work during which time I read Solzhenitsyn's *One Day in the Life of Ivan Denisovich*. Even though my head is floating near the ceiling and I can't swallow food, I'm aware that I can't waste time. I quiver with adrenaline. Every moment must be used for self-improvement. I had always meant to read this book and I'm not so sick that I can't focus my eyes.

That poor old Ivan Denisovich had it tough. Things can't be so bad for me, really. I'm not living in a forced labour camp in temperatures that would freeze my blood. Dave and I have a semi-detached house with an open fire at the end of a cul-de-sac, and we have a view over rolling fields. We each have a car, and Dave has a motorbike. Our neighbour James is as geeky as us – he works in computers, writes fan fiction, practises Tae Kwon Do and he's as excited about the new Star Wars movie as we are.

By the time my doctor's appointment comes round, I've gone back to work. My work ethic goes so deep, I can't stop myself. Adrenaline lifts my limbs and forces me out the door like a marionette. My clothes are loose and my jeans slide down my hips because acting normal with my colleagues takes an enormous amount of energy and I've lost the ability to eat. Work is more stressful than usual because my memory is shot and my vocabulary has shrunk. But if I keep smiling, no one will know. White wonky teeth, bright happy Tara. I'm on the verge of disintegration, a woman made of sand, and the only thing holding me together is my skin.

Sitting in the waiting room at the health centre, a poster featuring a family inside a heart makes me tearful. I can't look at the other patients – red-faced babies and young mums and elderly folk – they are breaking my heart. I wish I were at home. I don't want to see the doctor; people here have real problems – sick babies, poverty, abusive relationships, grief, decline, encroaching death. The doctor will look at my clear skin and bright eyes and think I'm an over-indulged, self-obsessed timewaster. Yes dear, she'll think, now go get a proper illness and come back when I can do something for you. I want to go home. I want to run for it. But Dave asked me to phone him after the appointment to tell him how it went, and I can't say I didn't go. He needs me to see the doctor.

The receptionist calls my name and I open the door to Dr Taylor's surgery, my legs aching, feet trailing, wondering what I'm going to say. A tired-looking woman in a pale polyester suit glances up from a desk.

I smile. Oh for God's sake, Tara, look like you feel. If I look like I feel I will lie down on the floor, slither below her table and stay there for a long time.

'Yes...' Dr Taylor says, looking at my file for my name. 'Tara.'

I sit down at the side of her desk. This kind of layout is supposed to encourage co-operation and avoid confrontation. I read that somewhere.

'I just wanted to get checked out for...' I don't know where to begin. 'I have... sore legs.'

Jesus.

'OK.' The doctor puffs as she leans over. 'Just roll up your trouser legs there.'

I roll up my jeans and say it's my knees and ankles. They feel loose, like they're made of water. She squeezes and prods.

'Anything else?'

'Well, I haven't been feeling... right.'

'In what way?'

Do I just come out and say I want to kill myself? Not every moment of every day, but more than the average person, I suspect. She would find it hard to believe anything so dark is going on inside my well-coiffed head. How do I explain that a week ago I completely lost my marbles? I'm functioning again now, although I'm made of water and everyone is judging me. I guess there's nothing wrong with me now. I can hardly believe it myself, how can I expect her to believe it?

'I've lost a lot of weight...' I say. I also have a fixed smile when I talk to people like you, Dr Taylor, people I want to like me, in fact, I want everyone to approve of me, to think I'm marvellous, and I'm torn apart if they don't. I know this is stupid, but I can't stop it. Is that a problem you can solve?

She asks me to pop on the scales. 'Any problems going to the toilet?' she says.

All my internal organs are wound tight like spools – my lungs, liver, spleen, intestines, ovaries, everything is in a knot. But all I say is, 'I can't poo.'

'OK. Let me just take your blood pressure.'

We sit down and I roll up my sleeve so she can place the cuff round my arm. She pumps, then nods at the result. Basically, I'm in the rudest of health.

'Well,' she sighs. 'I don't think there's anything physically wrong.'

I bury my face in my hands. Tears have snuck up on me. Everything is wrong. I struggle to get back in control.

She hands me tissues.

'Do you think you might be depressed?' she says.

Uhm.

I don't know. I'm not exactly sure what being depressed is. Don't I have to be really creative or something? I am creative, but I'm not cutting off my ear or drinking myself to death.

'Do you ever think of harming yourself?'

I think of slicing off my own skin with a kitchen knife. I think of the night of my book launch and how I wanted to die when I got home, how I am coiled so tight, every moment I am conscious hurts, and the only relief my body can offer is a vision of turning itself off.

'Yes,' I say.

She turns away and begins to write. 'Well, if you were going to kill yourself, you wouldn't admit it. You'd just do it.' She scribbles on a prescription pad. 'Put thoughts of suicide out of your head, they're silly. Start on these. They might make you feel a bit nauseous as your body gets used to them, but after a few weeks you should start to notice a difference. If they don't work, come back and we'll try a different one. It can take a few tries to find the right one. Make another appointment for six weeks' time and we'll see you then.'

And then I am outside in the car park, holding my prescription for Cipralex like a talisman. I'm not sure what just happened. That was like climbing to the top of a huge mountain only to come down the other side on a slide. And if she's right, then it looks like I can't even kill myself properly. I really am crap. Still, I'm relieved. I have an illness with a name, and I have tablets for it. Please, please, let them work, let them make me shiny and brilliant again.

I call Dave and let him know I have a thing called depression and I have a prescription. I tell him things the doctor didn't tell me – it happens to lots of people, it's just that people don't talk about it.

I hear the relief in his voice. A diagnosis means treatment, a prescription means everything will be back to normal again soon. I look up depression on the internet. I recognise everything, from the mysterious pains, to the sleeplessness, to the slow thinking, detachment, anguish and suicidal thoughts. And so many people on so many different drugs, complaining how they've been depressed for years, that the drugs don't work, that life continues to be shit and no one cares.

I have officially joined the world of the mad. Not the dazzling, dizzying madness of Van Gogh or Stephen Fry, just the catchall workaday madness of hopeless internet people.

Visible friends

'Why don't you go see that girl who lives up the road? Wee Sal?' my mother said.

Sal was older than me and had gone to Whitehead High too. She had her own flat in Rathcoole, a short distance from my mum's partner's house.

At my age, my mother was already married and had a child, with another on the way. Not that she wanted that for me; she just knew it was time I got on with life, met someone, moved on. When I finally emerged from my hibernation, I spent all my time with her and my sisters and their young children, where it was easy and comfortable and comforting. I was stalling.

She kept asking, gently, if any friends from Art College had been in touch, or if there were any friends from school I could arrange to see. None of them would want to see me, I was sure. They had lives now, I had been left behind. There was a girl my age living three floors below me, but she didn't even acknowledge me. I put it down to my repulsiveness and uncoolness, although with hindsight, she was probably just shy. As for Sal, I hardly knew her, and it would be weird just inviting myself along to her flat.

I signed on at 'the bru', the one where my father had signed on and I had stood outside vomiting. I was curious about claiming benefits, what the people were like in the queues, what the interview would be like. I told the bespectacled man behind the counter that I was happy to work at anything, although I had been to Art College so something creative might be good. I was beginning to feel like myself again. Alone in the flat, I read and wrote, but I didn't draw. I only did one more drawing after Art College, one of Dave that still sits in our living room, but drawing was over for me. I was also trying to teach myself to cook: boil in the bag spaghetti Bolognese, Tilda microwave rice with tinned tuna and pineapple, and pasta with salad cream (just once, not recommended). There were plenty of things I could do on my own.

My mother kept suggesting I meet up with wee Sal. She was persistent, to the point where she told Sal I would call up to see her. Aaargh! Feeling sheepish and under duress, I knocked on wee Sal's door. This was just weird, like going on a blind play date. This was not how friends were made. Still, Sal was welcoming, made me a terrible cup of coffee and we talked about what we'd done since school. In my case, fail at pretty much everything. In her case, work as an assistant in an architect's office with a boss she snogged at office parties.

Sal lived in a flat above a maisonette, but there were no evil kids in the immediate vicinity. Her place was hippyish, with throws and cushions and twinkly lamps, and books, magazines and records scattered around, Led Zeppelin's Houses of the Holy the permanent soundtrack. Half-hippy, half-punk, wee Sal was about five feet tall with long, sometimes red, sometimes blonde hair, a tiny turned-up nose and massive dark blue eyes. When she laughed, she threw back her head so you could see the dimple in her chin. She enjoyed the odd joint and wrap of speed and asked did I partake. I said yes, please.

Sal introduced me to her friend Lorraine, who worked in another architect's office and who was going out with a guy who rode a motorbike, and to Lynn, a vegetarian who wore little round glasses and was in love with James Hetfield from Metallica. Lynn had a younger brother with a raft of good-looking friends, and bizarrely, all these people were from Rathcoole. I had never seen them before, although hardly surprising when I'd spent the last decade in my room or on a bus. Even more bizarrely, they were normal people who did not throw stones, tell me I was ugly, or try out their flying kicks on me. I lived in constant wonder.

We started going to a pub a few miles away on Saturday nights, where Lorraine's boyfriend drank strong German beer with his mates. My mother smiled encouragingly when I told her about all the 'normal' things I was doing. I secured a part-time job in a video store (I'm not sure what the link was to creativity, but that's 'the bru' for you), and while it wasn't the great success my mother and I had imagined, it got me out of the flat, which was a start.

There was a handful of motorbikes parked outside the bar and inside, at the back, was a crowd, or rather a cloud, of darkness, which turned out to be Lorraine's boyfriend and his friends: edgy boys, with long hair in semi-dreads and plaits, a curious mix of pirate, native American and steampunk, who smoked and joked and rested their feet on their 'lids', which was, as Dave later explained, a helmet. From across the bar, they looked mildly threatening.

I wanted one.

A beautiful man

Dave's hair was long and blonde, curly at the ends, and scattered with plaits and beads. He had tanned skin and wore a Belstaff jacket, jeans held together with grimy patches, and a tattered scarf which he pulled up over his nose when he rode. He had unusual Teutonic features, which made him look even more exotic. For all their air of threat and potential for arrogance, the boys in the bar were laid-back, dope-smoking gigglers. Lynn's brother and his friends knew them, and we mixed without introductions.

I moved in on Dave like a predator. I don't know how it happened, or where the killer manoeuvre came from; it was not like me at all. Perhaps it was chemistry and hormones driving me like a raw and needy animal. When I noticed he was on his own, I slid in front of him and asked him if he'd been anywhere nice on his motorbike. He was gorgeous, he smelt like dust and earth, his stubble was ginger, I wanted to lick his face.

'Just back from Scotland,' he said.

'On holiday?' I asked.

'Yeah,' he said, and ran away.

Later, he told me he panicked. I wasn't like the other girls and he didn't know how to talk to me. Damn right I wasn't like them, but it was a long time before he found that out, and by then we were long married.

After some effort on my part, we finally arranged a date. He would take me to the north coast on his motorbike and we'd ride with two other couples – Lorraine and her boyfriend, and another of Dave's piratesque friends and his girlfriend who, it transpired, had gone to Whitehead High like Sal and me. I also learned that Dave was friends with Philip and Rob, the little boys I used to play with in Rathcoole before we moved to East Way. Philip and Rob rode motorbikes as well. This was all starting to feel strangely... right.

I wrapped my arms around him and squeezed him tight, almost stopping his breath as we rode along the Antrim coast. I pressed my helmet into his shoulder, nutting him in the back of the head every time he had to brake. I was dressed for the set of 'Happy Days', not a ride on a 1300cc Kawasaki, and my teeth chattered in the freezing wind. He thought I was pretty silly, but he didn't tell me that at the time. He bought me chips and a Coke in Portrush, we went to the amusement park, then he brought me home. I hadn't known such uncomplicated, good old-fashioned fun for such a long time. It was marvellous. Although no one said marvellous, they said 'cool'. Everything was, 'like, cool'. And when they said 'like', it sounded like luck.

Dave took life at a steady pace. He didn't over-think or second-guess or mindread the way I did. He wasn't striving to get ahead and he didn't have anything to prove. He was sexy and exotic and easy. He rode motorbikes and mountain bikes and jet skis, and did other fun things I hardly knew existed. But more than that, he was kind. He talked to me without expectation or judgement, and was interested in what I said. My love of books and writing was unusual to him, but that's what made me exotic too. He introduced me to Stiff Little Fingers and Frank Zappa, and put up with my favourites, Nick Drake and Tom Waits.

He says he loved me instantly. I've never been sure whether to believe him, but he is adamant. It took a little more time than that for me, but when I did realise I loved him, it hit me with a clunk and I couldn't let him go. As long as we were together, even if we were just staring out the window together, we were exquisitely happy. We were in love, made for each other, mad for each other.

It takes all kinds of crazy

After a year working at the video store and in a bar, and spending all my free time with Dave, I was ready to try education again. I was tired of living in clothes from Freeman's catalogue and walking the vanguard of crazies in the flats. In the video store, children stole empty video cases, pissed on the door and spat at the staff. In the bar, patrons fell over, passed out, pissed their pants and chatted me up. Something steely was forming inside me, a hard grit that wasn't there before. My mother and I still dreamed of the big house, the pots of money, the beautiful children, over our cappuccinos and caramel squares. All I had to do was pick the right route, one that wouldn't lead to a dead end. We believed that a degree would lead to a good job, which would lead to the good life.

Dave worked in engineering in Belfast, so I applied to universities in Northern Ireland. I was accepted onto the BA in English at Queen's University, which sounded wonderful, and I was offered a place on the BSc in Communication, Advertising and Marketing at Ulster University, which sounded lucrative. I would love every minute of studying for a degree in English, but how could that lead to a job? What would I do, work in a library? They'd probably put me in the library in the same estate I was trying to get out of. My mother felt that the BSc in Communication, Advertising and Marketing was probably the better bet. The description in the UCAS booklet said it had close links to industry and students spent a year working to gain experience and develop contacts.

Goodbye, joyous exploration of English literature, and hello money, money, money.

By the time I started my degree, I was considered a 'mature student', even though I was only two years older than most other students. The university was right. I wasn't like the giddy first year students, sprung fresh from good homes on the County Down coast, with their one hundred pound shoes and silky self-confidence. I befriended two older students who challenged and complained to lecturers, squeezed zits in the loo and wet themselves with giggles. I couldn't resist their self-deprecating silliness. When asked to illustrate her answer in a psychology assignment, one of them drew a picture of a rat. We still wet ourselves over that.

Dave moved into a flat with me and worked while I studied. I did almost no writing of my own. Evenings, when I would normally have written, were spent staring at Dave, pawing at Dave, holding Dave's hand, listening to music with Dave, playing cards with Dave and watching sci-fi with Dave. We were so in love, so wet, and when I see people in love, I think of how we were and smile. By the time I graduated, having spent a year working for a magazine, Dave and I were ready to get married. As the description of the course promised, I did make contacts, and it was one of these that landed me my first job as a Trainee

Advertising Planner in an ad agency in Belfast. I was on my way.

They paid me less than you would pay a donkey to take tourists up a hill. When was the money supposed to start rolling in? I worked long hours, and with no real training ('Read that, darling, then plan a creative strategy for this important client'). I learned quickly and on my feet. The bosses drove quality cars with leather interiors that soaked up their pungent perfumes. There was no middle management; there were the juniors who did the grunt work and the bosses who owned the business, pitched for work, took clients drinking in Dublin, shooting in Gleneagles and partying at the Barcelona Grand Prix.

Sitting with my boss in her perfumed Porsche on the way to a meeting in Dublin, she asked me what make-up brand I bought. Guerlain? Chanel?

I probably earned less money than she spent getting her blouses dry-cleaned over the course of a year. I blinked at her. I said I changed about it a bit, didn't have a favourite, then asked what she wore. I don't remember what she said, but I would imagine it was made from the magic dust that falls from cherubs' heads and was given to her free by a magazine wishing to curry favour.

The jump I made every day from penury to high-end luxury was disorientating. It was the 1990s and everything was designed to make clients feel special: designer furniture, fragrant air, thick chocolate biscuits on the boardroom table, luxurious gifts and trips. I had two pairs of trousers, three tops, two pairs of shoes, one bra, a plastic handbag and a big weekly repayment to Freeman's catalogue. I pretended to clients that I knew about rugby and holidays and expensive shops, and that I had a posh boyfriend with a swish car and wealthy parents, and that my bra wasn't held together with grey thread. If we juniors didn't swank up, we were told we were 'not very agency'.

My bosses were lucky, not just because they worked in the industry at a time when charisma, gifts and glossy pictures were often enough to win an account, but because they had recruited a bunch of bright, resilient young people who had no experience and no confidence, and who were keen to produce quality work with little in return. Because we received no feedback – no praise, no real criticism – we didn't know if our work was good. The bosses took what we created and sold it on. We decided that if the work made us laugh, then it was good. We laughed a lot, but that may have been delirium.

I made the move across to copywriting two years later, replacing the original copywriter who left to work in Scotland. Again, no real training ('Spit a couple of scripts out there, dollface. Important client's in at three'). Because I understood how people, or rather, 'consumers', thought, and I knew how to write, I ended up writing more than just radio scripts and long copy. I wrote tender proposals, which were normally written by senior staff. And still I was paid a very low salary. Not that I blame the bosses. They were good businesspeople and I presented them with an opportunity. I believed I wasn't particularly good when, in fact, I was. There was money to be made in that gap.

Something clicks

Three years in and I could feel myself sinking. I had worked hard, but I was still living in the flat in Rathcoole. I went from being ambivalent about my job – from hanging in there and hoping for progress – to dreading it. Advertising is where people end up when they have something to prove and that makes them exploitable. I was beginning to suspect I was good at my job, but I didn't have the confidence to do anything about it. If I went to another agency, they would clearly see I was a fraud. Job descriptions said they wanted go-getting, exciting, dynamic, motivated, confident, show-stopping superstars with mind-blowing portfolios. That wasn't me. I wasn't proud of the work I did; I very much doubted it was anywhere near mind-blowing. I wasn't even a real copywriter, I was just the girl who was filling in for the guy who went to Scotland.

Dave started working nightshift, which meant I was on my own in the evenings. I had picked up a second-hand Mac from work and was using it to put together my CV. I could give a good account of myself on paper, giving my career the kind of polish I might give a new dairy product or a shopping centre, but once an employer met me, they'd see straightaway I didn't know what I was doing. They would find me out.

God, it was boring in the evening without Dave. All our friends were couples now and many had young families. Almost none had gone to university, and I assumed they would think I was an intellectual snob or at the very least, too big for my boots. I was bored and restless at night, and miserable at work. Days and nights were too long. Reading used to make me happy, but reading wasn't enough. I didn't draw any more – that was for kids. (You have a lot to answer for, John Dickhead.) There was always writing, but I hadn't written anything in years. Out of curiosity, I opened up a new document and went to visit Fitzy.

My mother had suggested Dave and I start a family. Children made her happy, maybe they would do the same for me. She was probably right. We should start a family – we didn't have anything else to do.

Fitzy came out on the page a mix of Fitzy the punk and Fitzy the wild child. He had a girlfriend of sorts, now. Wow. And she was anorexic. Well, who woulda thought?

My salary had gone up £2.5k in two and a half years and Dave was in a steady job. This was as good as it was going to get. My expectations had been unrealistic to start with. A big house, pots of money. Pah.

Fitzy had a brother, but still no parents, poor guy. Oh well, much better off without them, I say. He plays guitar. Isn't he sweet? Eugh, I don't like sweet. Let's make him contemptible and contrary.

But starting a family because there was nothing better to do wasn't a great reason. Starting a family because you hadn't succeeded at anything else, wasn't that a bit, you know, Plan Z? Especially when you weren't in the least bit maternal. If you gave birth to a John Dickhead or a Hilda Wanky, you couldn't hide from them in your room, you were stuck with them. And what about all that drive and determination to escape and be successful? Could you really just turn it off?

In Fitzy's room, the sheets on his camp-bed were grey and sour. Candlelight disguised most of the mess.

No, I couldn't turn it off. It was stuck in my gullet and it got me through the shittiest days. There would be an escape from monotony and poverty and crazy cabbage-tossing people and rich people with no grasp of reality; somewhere, somehow, there would be something gloriously, wonderfully better, even if I couldn't see it yet. It was more nebulous than a big house and pots of money – it was about progress and betterment and achievement – and it had formed a nugget at my core. It was grafted into my workings and I couldn't turn it off.

What a rotten world Fitzy lived in, how much fun it was to take all my grim experiences and make them his. I could weave all my frustrations, observations and fantasies into his story. I'd forgotten how good this felt.

The more I wrote, the more I wanted to. I began to write each night while Dave was at work. I wasn't bored any more, I was having a great time. I could even work on the story if there was downtime in the agency.

Ah, this was the life. This was brilliant. Still no money, but I was happy. The only problem was that it wasn't my life, it was Fitzy's life I was enjoying. The life I had hoped for was still waiting for me somewhere.

But what if…

What if writing got me there?

That was it. I should take this writing thing seriously, put everything into it, stop pissing about and do it properly. This was where my drive and determination should be applied. I should write a novel and get it published. Yeah! I had absolutely no idea how to do it. But I had absolutely no doubt I would do it. Determination would get me there. I got up from the computer and ran my hands into my hair. This was IT. Oh my God.

I was a year and half away from my 30th birthday. I'd already wasted too much time. Starting a family could wait.

Dreams come true

Money doesn't make you happy, but neither does endless, grinding poverty. I didn't want pots of money – just enough so that I could buy a bra when I needed it, or a bit of make up when I ran out. And most of all, I wanted to buy a house in a nice quiet area where people didn't fire guns on communal stairwells. Dave and I longed for our own house, with a garage for Dave to tinker in and a garden for me to... I didn't know what I'd do in the garden, but my namesake Vita Sackville-West gardened, and I liked the idea.

We bought a car on a hire purchase-rental agreement and spent Sunday afternoons 'fantasy house-hunting', as we called it. County Antrim's narrow hawthorn-lined roads and soft green hills were strewn with beautiful homes – some were grand detached houses presumably owned by gazillionaires, others were cottages with histories crammed under their greying thatches. A cottage would do. Or a mansion. This was fantasy, you could have what you wanted.

With no savings and low incomes, we were delighted to hear about a government body who paid the deposit on your new home, and who you paid back when you earned enough. We secured a semi-detached new-build on the outskirts of Carrickfergus and watched its construction from field up. We recorded its early life the way other people record their child's; we took photographs of its breezeblock skeleton, its first roof tiles, the gaps for its windows and doors. I have a picture of my mother posing by an imaginary hearth in the breezeblock living room with her hand on an imaginary mantelpiece.

As the house developed, so did the novel about Fitzy. I carried my work-issue laptop in and out of the agency every day, making it easier to write. I could just open the computer wherever I was and start, without even opening a document. Every spare moment was spent working on the book: lunchtimes, in between jobs in the agency, at home in the evening. I had no time to waste. I would be thirty soon, and if I wasn't successful by the time I was thirty, I was sure there would be no hope for me. Every other successful person in the world had triumphed long before he or she was thirty. I might just scrape in. I wrote with great urgency, but with it came new energy. I started a new healthy-eating regime and began to lose weight. My skin glowed, I felt energised, and the more I wrote, the more energy I had.

Acceleration

They knew at the agency I was writing a book: they could see me working on it when the office was quiet, but rather than give anyone the opportunity to accuse me of slacking off, I pushed myself harder, coming up with bigger and better ideas, writing funnier and cleverer scripts, and taking on a key role in pitches and presentations. They started to pay me more. Heavens above. When I had desperately wanted money, it didn't come. Once I'd focused on something else, it came in lumps. Someone up there was on my side at last.

I began to feel like a kind of conduit. I wasn't controlling the writing – it was flowing out of me. All kinds of connections and ideas were falling onto the page and I wasn't in charge. Inspired by East Way, a dog-eat-dog motif grew until the whole book was bound up in it: Fitzy was renamed Cuchulain, after the mythic Irish hero also known as the Hound Of Ulster; in my book, he was called Cookie for short (a tasty morsel); Cookie's best friend Bonehead (made of tougher stuff) was attacked by a dog, later eaten up by the dogs of war. I was on fire. I found I had even more energy: I could write until the wee hours, wake up laughing and be a superstar in work. Dave and I started going out mid-week to see punk bands play in Belfast and we got up the next day and carried on. Dave cut off his long hair and bleached it blonde and looked incredibly hot. I got a quirky new hairstyle for my thirtieth birthday. And I bought bras... loads of them!

Encouraged by my mother, I sent a few chapters and a synopsis to an Irish publisher. My mother was happy to see us so happy, but we were better than that. We were flying. We were having the best time ever – Dave said he had never seen me so happy. No wonder. I was right on the crest of a manic high. It was wonderful.

300mph

The world ran on coincidences. My photograph was in a local magazine. On the next page was the commissioning editor from Blackstaff Press who, within days, would ring to say she loved my writing and wanted to talk to her colleagues about offering me a deal. Dave's workmate had told him his girlfriend worked for a publisher, and she'd found this really good book in the slush pile, unlike anything she'd read before – didn't Dave's wife write? His girlfriend was the commissioning editor who had contacted me. It was my book. It was weird.

I would read a word in a newspaper and hear it on the radio at the same time. I would think of someone and they would turn the corner and appear in front of me. Dave and I would ring each other at exactly the same time. Ideas formed into seamless things without command. I was buzzing. I just had to open my mouth and clever stuff would come out. Jesus. I could do anything. Why had I never been like this before? Why had it taken so long to get this way? It didn't matter – now I had the energy to make up for it.

The publisher offered me a deal and wanted the book completed within four months – did that work for me? I said I was re-writing it and working full-time, but four months would be fine, I would make it work. I wasn't going to endanger this; I would give them exactly what they wanted.

I could keep up the pace no problem. Because this was IT. This was my chance. I had to make this work, I had to make this book brilliant and perfect and smart and creative and original and all the different things that whizzed around my head at 300mph, and I had to do it now. Every dead-loss hope, every big house and pots of money dream, every ounce of fuckery I ever wanted to leave behind was wrapped up in this book. I would make it work if it killed me.

I worked harder, longer, honing and shaping and writing and re-writing. We partied hard, drank too much, ate too little. I was living at breakneck speed and I was dragging Dave with me. The agency was thriving, and I became the boss's pet, making her ideas sing, impressing everyone with my speed, skill and energy. We won bigger accounts and created higher profile campaigns. I started receiving gifts – a monogrammed leather Filofax, champagne, trips away with clients, awards.

And then. Sometimes. My legs would shake. I would look down at my knees and they felt like water. I could see my bones clearly through my jeans. And my brain was still working, working, working. Wasn't eating weird? You used your hand to transfer stuff to your mouth, whereupon it disappeared inside you. INSIDE YOU! Big brands should build houses. You should be able to buy a Virgin House or an apartment on an Ikea street. It could be a franchise, builders could buy into it. I could run a magazine. Or a bookshop, or a café-bookshop, with a dance floor.

We'd have tea dances during the day for old folk, salsa early evening, a nightclub later on. The waiting staff would know how to dance and they'd get people up to teach them. Let's grow vegetables. I can't dig, I'm too tired.

Crash

I can't do this anymore.

It was a quiet voice. Not Dave, not anyone else; the voice was inside me. And it wasn't the new me or the old one. It was small, quiet, distinctive, like something true and weighty in the middle of an empty room the size of a hall. Words I could hear, see and feel.

I can't do this anymore.

I ignored it. Carried on.

I began to hear it when I worked on the book at night and when I worked on campaigns during the day. I shocked everyone, including myself, when I started to cry in a presentation to a client. I wondered if I should tell Dave. The voice was getting stronger and it was getting more upset. It was making me upset. It was becoming my voice.

I can't do this anymore.

I kept going. Working, partying, smiling.

We needed an idea for a big pitch; every agency in town would be competing for this new advertising account. It was worth a lot of money over three years and I wanted to win, not because I was competitive, but because that kind of account kept people like me in jobs. I was the ideas person and I was clearly on a roll. What did I think? What was my Big Idea? I scrambled around inside my brain, but it was cavernous and empty. I had nothing.

The team met to discuss how we would approach the pitch. Feeling doom-laden and shaky, I sat down at the glossy board table amid general chitchat and waited for everyone to join the meeting.

A colleague asked me casually, 'So which publisher is publishing your book?'

I told him.

'Oh, that's the publisher for one-hit wonders,' he sneered.

Was it? Or was he jealous? No, he was right. I wouldn't, couldn't, do this again. I was empty. The book was a one-off. I wasn't a writer, I worked in advertising. I didn't know what I was doing. The book was coming together, but it wasn't anywhere near good enough. I needed more time. And yet I longed for the deadline because I was desperate to stop. Stop everything. Stop working, stop thinking, stop partying stop stop stop.

The way to stop was to die.

The pitch team was ready – we had our project plan, we knew who was doing what, we had dates in our diaries. All we needed now was the idea. My idea. I was dispatched to 'ideate'. It never occurred to me to tell anyone I was falling apart.

Wheels come off

Review copies of an early draft of my novel *Fodder* were sent out and I panicked. Critics were reading my dirty laundry. The draft was full of holes, the characters unfinished, the language uncrafted. It had to sound like poetry, every single word, but it was clunky and arrhythmic. Critics were being asked to review a piece of shit. Why couldn't they let me finish it first? They couldn't wait for me to finish – review copies would go out in advance.

We argued over the front cover. I don't like to argue, but I hated their ideas. What the hell was wrong with these people? I was being 'awkward'. Every publisher's nightmare. An author who wants to control every last thing. Who does she think she is? I knew I wasn't good enough for them, I wasn't like their other authors, *real* writers. The editor who selected my book had moved on. No one believed in the book. It was disastrous.

The media were interested: TV, radio, newspapers, readings, panels, signings, the launch night. People, so many people, asking questions, wanting to know everything about me, all judging, looking for fault.

'Where are you from?'

I kept it vague: from Co Antrim/Carrickfergus/Belfast/undefined; *not* Rathcoole, where paramilitaries rubbed shoulders with people who had no noses and dropped cabbages from heights, where good kids could get eaten up and where my mother still lived. I was terrified someone would take offence at what I'd written and smash the windows of her partner's house.

'What do your parents do, are they writers too?'

Ha ha ha, if only you knew. I said my mother encouraged me to read from babyhood, propping me up with a book in the pram. It was true, but of course, it didn't answer the question as it was asked. I was getting good at that.

'Would you sign my book?'

'You read so well!'

'That was funny, I loved it!'

When I knew they were really saying, who does she think she is, does she think she's better than us?

Every second was spent smiling, every second was excruciating.

The book was full of the language I learned in East Way and there I was, on primetime TV, promoting it. The poor old ladies! Don't let them read it. Hide it hide it hide it!

Dying, though. Dying.

BBC Radio 3 commissioned me to write something – 'Anything at all, Tara, we love your work' – to read in front of an audience for an arts programme that would play out the following week.

On the night I was due to read this new work, Dave and I stood outside the beautiful old red-bricked venue that had been booked for the event. Alarmingly posh London producers rushed about in corduroy and lamb's wool, saying 'wof awf fhnahf wof' in accents that left me petrified.

I smoked and shook in my shoes. I was made of sticks, rattling together inside my clothes. Around us, elm trees cast off their leaves and the world was dying around me.

I was an oik, I didn't belong there. I should leave. Writers were weird, they sloped off and got drunk all the time. The best ones did that, I should do that. But I couldn't. My steely work ethic, my need for approval, my desire not to let any opportunity pass me by – they glued me there. My only escape would be dying.

I read my story to a small audience and received some applause. They were patronising me, obviously. The presenter asked me questions I couldn't answer. I confused myself, I didn't make sense. I was making this difficult for him. I sat on a panel with poets, novelists, *real* writers, to discuss an impenetrable poem written by the much-lauded poet sitting right beside me, and who was obviously looking down at me. I told them all, giggling, that I had no idea what the poem was about. Really, don't ask me, I wouldn't know. I didn't belong there. I made a dick of myself. Dave and I should have gone drinking instead.

'That was awful, Dave, *awful*,' I said, as I hurried from the venue, dragging him behind me. I twisted in anguish. Dying was the only way.

'It wasn't *that* bad,' he said. He was, of course, being kind.

Reviews of the novel came in, some people loved it, some missed the point, others clearly hadn't read it. One critic called me a 'middle-class lassie' and I realised the integrity of the work was compromised because I wouldn't say where I was from. It looked like I'd made up the madness, that I had no idea what it was like to live sub-class. After all my efforts, I'd done it wrong. Every bit of criticism, even good criticism, hit me hard. My insides were riddled with holes where their words punched though.

At a trade launch organised by the publisher, I found myself standing beside an older female author selecting canapés from a buffet table. How smiley we were, how fiercely nice. I picked at vol-au-vents and eggy things I had no appetite for.

'It's different these days,' she told me. 'People only get published because they're blonde and easy on the eye.'

Did she mean me? Was that an insult? Or a compliment? Whatever it was, I suspected she was right. I wasn't a writer. *Fodder* proved I didn't know anything about writing. I had shown everyone how rubbish I was. I was an ignorant, deluded oik and I had fucked up the one thing I thought would save me.

I had failed.

Meanwhile, the agency still needed an idea for the big pitch, but there were no ideas inside me. I told them it was about dreams. When I was asleep, I saw God.

Dying was all that was left.

Tara West

In the dark

Tara West

Descent

What is the fucking point in keeping a journal? A dialogue with myself? I don't know what I'm fucking talking about. I don't even want to listen to me. I want to shut myself down. I want to bash my face on the end of the bed.

That's an excerpt from the journal I kept at the time, on the advice of the many, many books I read on depression, none of which I can remember because my memory wasn't working. Anyone I was introduced to that year – a new client or a writer – speaks to me like they know me, and often I have only the loosest idea of who they are and what our relationship is. Depression affects your memory, but in addition to that, I was heavily doped up on anti-depressants. But I can't tell them that or ask them to re-introduce themselves. I sometimes wonder if I should apologise for doing anything weird when we first met. I can't even begin to talk to them about it.

It's probably easier to say you steal from charity shops or road-test lube than tell someone you have been, or are, depressed. To say you are suicidal in the off-the-cuff manner in which you actually feel it can be deeply shocking to other people. They find it hard to accept and believe. It's too big, too dramatic

The other reason depression is hard to talk about is that no one can see it, so it's not easy for others, and often the sufferer, to accept that there's anything wrong. You look the same. There's often no hint outside of the tortuous goings-on inside. You may even look like you're having the time of your life. You can put up an extremely good front, which is what I did for six weeks after my breakdown. But it doesn't last – one way or another, you'll crack.

I went back to work after my breakdown and pretended I was still bright and shiny, that everything was fine, that I was still their superstar. I failed. To be fair, manic activity sets the bar very high. That level of creativity couldn't be maintained, and yet it was still expected of me – I had proved I could do it. I had skills, formulae, set phrases and templates I could fall back on, material I could cut and paste, but it was gone. My brain was still hammering along at 300mph, but it was focusing on the wrong things. I couldn't generate fresh ideas, build arguments or remember words. Rather, I tore myself apart from the inside out.

I believed everyone was against me, scheming, talking, denigrating. I thought that my boss hated me, that the clients thought I was strange and inarticulate. During meetings, I would float away and watch the conversation like I was a shadow in the room. If they only knew I've lost my marbles, I'd think. To them I looked like I always did and yet I was shifting like tectonic plates, there was nothing solid about me. I was shrinking by the day, expending huge amounts of energy trying to appear normal, while fighting extremes of mood and thought.

I told a friend in work what was happening, and she insisted I go back to the doctor. But I didn't think I could. I'd just been to the doctor and I needed to give the anti-depressants time to work. I wasn't one for demanding attention about health problems, I dealt with them and moved on. But in the end, I gave in. I was getting worse. I was paranoid to the point where I could barely walk down the street for feeling that everyone was watching and pointing. I cringed and cowered all day. I couldn't hold a conversation, I couldn't go into shops. The library, a favourite haunt, was a no-go area. They might ask about my book and I found the book excruciating. I couldn't switch off day or night, managing on about four hours' sleep. I hummed with adrenaline and I had a sick and nervy energy that stopped me from relaxing:

I cleaned the outside of the kitchen cupboards, and the inside, threw out some rubbish, blackened and polished the grate, watered the plants, bleached the kitchen floor, shifted bookshelves, cleaned a few mirrors and tidied. I don't have the concentration to read and I'm not doing a good job of writing either. I feel pulled in twenty different directions at once. I have the feeling you get when you have to get up early to travel and your face feels numb the rest of the day. I might clean the living room floor.

Dr Taylor wasn't available, so I made an appointment with Dr Corr, my mother's GP. She was probably only a few years older than me, with soft brown eyes, a quiet voice and a gentle sense of humour. Propelled by that same unpleasant energy, I talked fast and uncontrollably. I looked at the clock on the surgery wall. I had overstayed my allotted time, but it didn't seem to bother Dr Corr.

In her measured voice, she said Cipralex seemed to be increasing my anxiety and she changed my prescription to Zispin. Side effects were sleepiness and weight gain, but she said it sounded like I needed help with sleep, and I looked underweight anyway. If I put on more weight than I was comfortable with, I could always lose it when I felt more on top of things. She printed out some information on depression and the new medication, and said she would put my name forward for counselling. I should come back to see her in six weeks, but before that if I was worried.

The day after my appointment with Dr Corr, I finally told my mother what was happening. I had been pretending all was fine for too long; I wanted the comfort she could provide, and it was a relief to come clean. Now that Dave and I had our own house, I saw her every Saturday. We would go grocery shopping in the afternoon and afterwards she would come to my house and we would drink coffee and eat caramel squares in the small, comfortable living room.

She had always had problems with blood pressure and now she had heart disease and was taking a daily handful of drugs to manage it. In the days before my breakdown, Dave would frequently hear my mother and I laughing over our coffee and caramel squares while he was in the garage tinkering with his bike. I was worried about telling her, not just because she was ill herself, but because I thought I would disappoint her. I had been doing so well, making a decent salary, moving to a nice area; all the things we had dreamt about seemed to be happening. And then, suddenly, they weren't. I was turning down promotional opportunities and readings because I couldn't bear the thought of talking to people or being looked at. It was getting harder and harder to walk from the front door to the car. I was terrified of meeting James next door, the nicest guy in the world. Whoever saw me would judge me, laugh at me, see me falling apart.

My mother was loving and supportive, held my hand and hugged me. I didn't tell her I felt suicidal. I wanted to protect her from that. I couldn't tell her I wanted to die, it would distress her so deeply, I just couldn't say it. She was not, as far as I could tell, disappointed. I realise now she could never have felt disappointment if one of her children were sick, but my skewed way of thinking always took the worst of what I believed and attributed it to the people around me.

Unchristmas

There are photographs of me on Christmas Day, two months after my book launch. I have started Dr Corr's new prescription and they have made me seasick. I look bizarre in the photographs. I am wearing a pink fleecy dressing gown, kneeling on the floor and holding the laptop computer Dave has just given me to write my next book (I did use it, eventually, eight years later, when it was a dinosaur of the computer world and I was finally able to write again). My neck is a stick, my face is grey, and my head is too big for my body. I am smiling the smile of an old woman who knows she must smile but can't remember why.

Dave and I spent Christmas Day on our own. I talked to my mother on the phone but I couldn't face the rest of my family or Dave's. He was fine with that, he just wanted me to be OK. We lit the fire and watched TV, but I couldn't concentrate. I was sure I was ruining his Christmas, being so feeble and nervous and limited. We were still affectionate, but sex had stopped, and I was worried he would think I didn't love him. And then I upset him when I told him that, because he thought I thought he only wanted me for sex, and that I believed he thought that was the sum of our relationship. I sobbed into his shoulder because I had hurt him. I was a danger to be around.

It was a very quiet Christmas. There was nothing good or light inside me, I had no opinions, nothing useful to contribute, and Dave, thankfully, didn't try to cheer things up. He was worried, but he was patient, and we sat on the settee and held hands without talking. The TV was on permanently to fend off the silence and when Dave went out to see his friends, I stared fretfully at the TV until he came back. I couldn't concentrate to read, and I couldn't listen to music because it made me cry.

The agency closed for a week and I hoped it would be long enough to get myself back together, but as the days wore on, nothing changed. The thought of going back worried at me like a dog gnawing a wound. A week was not enough to rebuild an entire person. I couldn't go back – the workload, the presentations, the people – it was like a kind of horror approaching on the horizon. I understood that people in warzones faced much worse than sitting on a leather chair in a nice office with a pink pebbled yard outside, but that didn't change how I felt. Something had kicked off in my head and I couldn't control my terror. The thought that I was suffering so badly over virtually nothing made me feel even worse.

What worried me most was that if I were going to take time off, I would have to tell my boss everything. The idea of speaking to her was huge and dreadful and began to dominate every day.

My boss would never believe there was anything wrong. I looked fine before Christmas. I looked totally agency. I was a drama queen, a lightweight, a skiver; depression was – well, what the hell was depression? It wasn't an easy thing to explain, but I would still have to explain it to her, when the illness itself had made me incoherent and cringing and full of self-doubt. I felt like a pencil balancing on its point in the middle of a void. It was a searing anguish, disproportionate to the reality.

I can read your mind

The night before I am due back at work, I sit on the bed beside the upstairs phone, my hands scrabbling over my jaw and mouth. I've learned to recognise this behaviour. It re-appears when I get hiccups in my thinking.

I call my boss at home.

Oh my God, the pleasantries! I forgot about these. Fuck! Must we open every conversation with, 'Hello, how are you?'

Because we must all say in return, 'I'm fine, how are you?'

Common decency and good manners have tripped me up. I'm already sounding normal. How can I expect her to believe I'm suffering from depression? And that my thinking is so extraordinarily distorted and painful, dying seems the only way to escape it?

'How was your Christmas?' she asks, merrily.

OK, right, so I'm ready now. No more pleasantries.

'Well, not too good,' I say. 'I haven't been very well over Christmas.'

Ah, here we go, I'm thinking she's thinking, an extended holiday, no one wants to come back to work after holidays, come on, it's so obvious. Thought you were better than that, Tara.

'Oh dear,' she says. 'Sorry to hear that.'

'So I won't be in tomorrow.'

'Alright. Well, when do you think you'll be back, do you know? Just so we can plan.'

'I'm not sure.' My chin is tucked into my chest and I'm quivering like a terrified rabbit. A rabbit who's been shot and caught in the headlights and jammed in the jaws of a large dog.

'Is it flu or something?' she asks.

'No, I...'

Silence. It sounds like I'm lying. THERE'S NOTHING WRONG WITH ME. This is so dodgy. Lying lying lying.

'I have depression.'

'Oh?' Which means 'explain please'. And possibly, 'So what?'

'You remember that day when I said my cold hadn't cleared up and I went home early?' I say.

'No.'

'I was off for a couple of days?'

'Oh, yes, yes.'

'Well, that was the day... I wanted to kill myself.'

Silence. The silence of held breath, of synapses firing and hitting walls.

I used to be able to build arguments, to manipulate words so the listener or reader was ready to accept my proposition before I actually delivered it. Not any more. As far as arguments went, that was a sack of shit dropped off a cliff.

'Oh,' she says, at last. 'Well, that's not good. Not good at all. Have you been to see the doctor?'

She's checking me out, to see if it's for real, to see whether I've diagnosed myself with a magazine article.

'Yes. I've got anti-depressants.'

'Are they working?'

'Yes.' I'm still detrimentally eager to please, but saying yes is a ridiculous overpromise, so I say, 'No.' But that seems like there's no hope for me, and I don't want to lose my job altogether, we have bills to pay, so I say, 'I don't know.'

I wish I could explain this better, do myself justice, and give her a chance to understand, but it's all a scramble and I'm sweating and I need to get off the phone because I might bawl, gracelessly, screamily, and it won't be very agency at all.

'You didn't really seem yourself before Christmas,' she says.

I'm glad she said that, because it gives kudos to my argument, but at the same time, what did she mean? Did she think I was weird, nuts, mental, egotistical, insubordinate, slacking, stupid, deluded, pathetic, silly, disgusting, smelly, a liar, a liability, *what*? *What did she think*?

'I thought you probably just needed a holiday,' she says.

'I did, I really did,' I say. And then I think, does that sound like the lady doth protest too much? It does. She thinks this is a ruse to take an extended holiday. I know she does. She thinks I'm lying. I'm not ill. I'm fine, nothing is broken or bleeding, I'm not vomiting, coughing or limping.

What made me think I could get away with this? I'm lazy, sly, skiving, conniving.

'OK, well, keep in touch,' she says. 'Can you send in a doctor's line?'

'I will.'

'OK, take care.'

'You too.'

I hang up and put my head on my knees. I fucked up. She thinks it's all lies. She's gone off now to tell her husband and they'll stare at each other knowingly. I've confirmed what they've suspected all along. Employees will always take the mick, even the ones you thought you could trust. They hate me.

My mind is twisted so tight I can't move from the bed. I can only sit there and wait for something awful to happen. When Dave comes to find me, my legs have seized up and I walk behind him like I've aged 60 years. He asks how it went and I say it went OK, everything is fine.

My boiler is bust

I got a doctor's line for two weeks, and then another three weeks, and another two weeks after that. I was off work from Christmas through to the end of February and my boss told the rest of the staff I had a viral infection. They paid me throughout and I was deeply grateful. My friend in work let me know everyone missed me, and my boss phoned occasionally to check in, telling me they missed me and my work and hoped I would be back soon. They were good to me, but in my deep and destructive mood, I quailed in terror each time she phoned, second-guessing and misreading her every word. I couldn't cope with anything or anyone. I stayed away from the windows, lived in dread of the phone and spent a lot of time in the bath imagining scraping my skin off with a knife. The slightest thing would prompt a greatly disruptive and disproportionate response. On Saturday 18th January, I wrote:

I was doing OK today. Dave got up about 3.30pm and I hung about in my jimmers until after 4pm. Then I went up and had a bath. I footered about with a book on stress management (I have a depressive personality type – conscientious, outwardly happy, blah, blah blah) and a book on the inner child, blah blah blah, then I made us tea and then the boiler broke down.

We lit the fire and Dave called his mum to find out about the man who moved their boiler for them and now he's coming down here after eight. And when I found that out, I burst into tears. I confessed to Dave that I can't cope with anything. Crying on his shoulder, I wanted to cry out for help, and yet I couldn't. Because he can't help me and I can't keep torturing him. I wanted to die, because I thought it would be so much easier. For me, for him.

I know it wouldn't. It would probably destroy him, but my thinking is all wrong and I NEED HELP. I cried in bed last night. I needed help. I don't know what that help is but I need it. I'm not getting out of this on my own.

Oh God, what am I going to do?

I think if the boiler hadn't broken down, I would have been fine. I had a good day and I was able to think – but now I know this man is coming, I am tense and anxious. I don't want to deal with anybody. Earlier I thought I would sleep well tonight because...

Mummy just phoned and now the boiler man is here. I started to cry with mummy on the phone. I'm annoyed at myself for doing that because that makes her feel awful but I couldn't hold it in.

I feel so bad and I don't know what to do. I need help.

I'm sure the boiler man wonders what's wrong with me, with my big tear-stained face. My hair's dirty too – but at least I don't smell.

Oh God I feel awful and I don't know what to do. It's not that I feel alone. It's that I feel desperate. I feel the same way I felt before I started on the anti-depressants – I feel very, very bad.

This is desperate. I don't know what to do.

I wish I could get some perspective on things. I wish I could run away.

I feel like I have backed myself into a corner and the only way out is to go through more pain.

To have come so far – and then to give it up. It wouldn't feel like relief – it would feel like quitting. Failing. Giving in.

The only alternative is to go on the way I'm going. To go back to work and just plough on. Maybe that's what I should do. Just try and get on with things.

Could I do that?

I don't know.

I'm lost.

Oh God I can't cry while the boiler man is here.

My stomach is in a knot and my legs are wobbly, but at least my shoulders aren't as stiff as they were.

Imagine getting into a state over the boiler man coming out. Christ. I've scared mummy now. I wish I didn't have to share this with her. Or Dave. Because it's not fair on them. I wish I could take myself away from them. I wish I wasn't doing this to them.

I just feel so desperate. And the awful thing is, I don't know why. I just feel like I'm losing it.

The boiler man has gone and I've since been on the phone to mummy and I apologised to her and to Dave for falling apart. God help them both.

A brutal place

I drove along the inland road to Carrickfergus with my mother beside me in the car. On either side of us, the fields were winter grey and the roadside hawthorns were twisted and bare. It was here that I realised my mother and Dave didn't deserve what I was doing to them and my death would make things easier for them.

I wrote in my journal:

Today I thought about suicide. If only to take the pain away from myself and the torture away from Dave and mummy. I know that torture would be even greater for them if I did do it, but I can't think right. And I know how deeply selfish it is to think this way, but if I wasn't here I wouldn't know. How dark it is. How dark how dark how dark.

I feel so awful and down it doesn't feel real. I feel like a plastic shell of myself, typing away at this machine, Stargate on the TV. So OK on the outside, so Tara-looking, and yet inside I've gone.

It's a painful job hanging on. It's tiring.

And I can't tell anybody because they would feel they had to do something to help, and they would be shocked and hurt. Mummy and Dave keep asking are you sure you're OK and I have to say yes because saying no would only hurt them more.

This has to pass. Has to. I can't go on like this.

Everything was lost to me – my reality, self, Dave, my mother. They stood by helplessly as I unravelled.

This is as strange as I've ever felt. I'm not real. I want to go get out.

Dave is upstairs having a bath. He took the night off work because I was in a state today. Mummy was here and we cleaned the windows and then the phone rang and I didn't want to answer it and mummy said answer it so I did and it was my boss. She said how are you and I said not too bad.

Which was a fucking pleasantry and she will have thought I am good.

I told her mummy was here and I couldn't really talk. I said did she want to meet up for a coffee or come down here so I've to phone her tomorrow again to arrange something.

Then afterwards I threw an absolute wobbler. I didn't want to talk to her. The timing was unbelievable. If the universe is trying to drive me over the edge, it is winning.

I told mummy I felt like I was cracking up. She held onto me but I couldn't feel anything. I fucking well howled. She wanted to phone to get the doctor out but I said I was OK. She thought maybe I should go into hospital. But I don't want to go into hospital. I don't know what I want. But I'm not right. I know I'm not.

I have left myself somewhere. This is how I felt on my very worst day. I think I'm getting worse. I'm not getting better.

I left myself somewhere. I can't tell Dave or mummy how I feel. That I think about dying a lot. That if it wasn't for them, I would go.

But they are so distant. On the other side of an invisible wall, even when I hug them. And I try to make them feel better but I'm losing it. I'm losing my ability to see things from another point of view. I've lost it. I've lost something. I'm lost.

I don't know what comes next after this. What can come next? I thought you couldn't get any lower than your lowest but I didn't know.

I wish the universe would fucking well help me out here. Help me out here! Come on!

This is shite shsihqewglWR#Ne#2ET'9U 3Q5 3i

I'm not at my lowest. You can push me further. But how far will I go? I won't hang on do you want my energy?

Was I treating you like a pet? Is that it? What the fuck do you want me to do? Do you want me back? The substance that I am. Just to fade into the nothing AGAIN TO START AGAIN. Not another person she'll only do the same. Surely.

Where can I go from here?

Show me.

Mummy says try a wee prayer. There. That was a prayer. You've got me now. What the fuck do you want me to do? Where am I supposed to go? What do you want me to do?

The only reason I want to go to bed is in the hope that I won't wake up. But I will and if it's the same I will have to die. I can't do this forever.

Nothing existed beyond the moment and the moment caused me the worst kind of mental pain, an anguish like the sharpest, rawest grief. I thought I was protecting Dave and my mother because I didn't tell them I wanted to die, but depression provides no shelter for loved ones. They suffered because of me.

Had they not been there, death would have been a release and a relief. I knew how I would do it. But when I thought about how my death would affect them, I couldn't do it. Without doubt, they saved me. But at the time, they prolonged my pain. I was caught between the desire to switch myself off and the need to keep going for their sakes. I was tormented.

Undead

I went back to the doctor at my mother's insistence. Dr Corr listened in her kind, patient way, but my explanation of how I was feeling didn't, couldn't, come close to the reality. Sedatives might have helped, but that kind of anguish is impossible to describe at 10am in a doctor's brightly-lit surgery. And perhaps Dr Corr was concerned I might use sedatives to the wrong end. She upped the dose of Zispin and by the end of January, I was a tearful zombie, numbed and struggling for lucidity.

Everything feels different. My house feels different. I feel more cut off from the neighbours than I ever have. I feel pointless. A blur. A mist in the shape of me. With no feelings. And tired. And sleepy.

Sometimes I think I want to die and then other times I worry that there's something wrong with me and I'm going to die. How fucked up is that? Sometimes I feel clear and can hear the birds outside and other times I disappear up inside my head so far, I can't see or hear or feel anything.

I've lost me again and this time I think I'm sad about it. Not angry. Not anxious. Resigned I suppose. I'm getting tired waiting to get back to normal and even though I tell myself – because I've read it in the literature – that things do change and

I will feel better, I don't really believe it. This is so shit.

I really want to run away. I can't bear the thought of going back to work feeling like this.

Room to ruminate

Zispin anaesthetised me. The pain was lessened because I lost the ability to focus on it. I felt heavier, lugging myself around like vulcanised rubber. I might have looked like I was in the room with Dave, staring at the TV, but I was just a shape. I don't remember anything we watched, and even today, a movie will come on and I'll suggest we watch it and he'll say we saw it years ago. I sat through entire sci-fi series and didn't know. After a month, when I was less distracted by pain, old and new anxieties flared up. Was my mother going to die? Was Dave having an affair? What about the book? Why did no one care? Why couldn't I write anymore? Could I handle the stress of work? Why was I like this? Would I be like this forever?

My journal pours over these questions in the most laboured, dreary and repetitive way, as though in my head I'm rocking in my seat, picking at wounds, pulling out hair, examining what they're made of in the most pointless and unhelpful detail. I was going round in self-absorbed circles and although Zispin was keeping me steady, it wasn't helping me up. I longed for someone to talk to, someone who would listen without judging me. Not my mother or Dave, who I wanted to protect, or friends, who would want to help (and who I was sure would still be thinking – but how can you be depressed when you've just had a novel published, you have a good job, a supportive husband, a lovely home, and you aren't dying of cancer or living in a warzone?)

I wondered about the counselling service Dr Corr had put my name down for and I mulled it over in my journal in the same grinding, useless way I examined all my other concerns. I even wrote an entire conversation between me and an imagined counsellor, in which we discussed my worries at length before I got angry, swore and stormed out on myself.

Fucuuuuuuuuck! You stupid stupid fuck. Fuck this fucken waste of fucken time this is shit. I fucken hate this it's shit. Why now? Why fucken now? Fuck you.

At the beginning of February, I received a letter from the counselling service telling me there were no appointments available at that time. It was a strange letter to send anyone – there was no indication of a waiting list, or recommendation of other routes I might try. I analysed it to death. Wasn't I sick enough? Wasn't I important enough? Did I live in the wrong area? Was I too much of a 'middle class lassie'? Was it because I drove myself to illness and didn't deserve help? The letter was such a dead end; not only did it disappoint me, it confused me. What was I supposed to do with this knowledge? What should I do next? Drift along as I was? I hated me, I hated my life, but I wasn't suicidal anymore. I was desperately unhappy, but medication had numbed me; I was enervated and depressed physically and mentally. What next? Anything? Or was that it?

I searched around online. Private counselling cost around £30 a session and I couldn't afford to pay that every week. I became increasingly frustrated, not just at the lack of help and direction I felt I was getting from the health service, but at the drain on my energy and my own lack of progress. I was angry at myself for being this way, for ruining everything, for taking away my own momentum. Being driven and independent, I thought if no one else was willing to help me get better, I would just have to do it myself. I wrote:

I made a decision as far as I am capable of making a decision.

God I hate the sound of racing on the TV. Any kind. Cars. Bikes. Horses. I hate it.

But that was not my decision.

I decided that I am the only one who can help me now. Who can turn me around. It will be self help in the most fundamental, non-new-age-jargon kind of way.

I can't wait any longer. I have to start making steps myself. And taking that decision has made me see that my illness has prevented me from making decisions. I more or less decided on self help last night, after I'd finished writing in here and had gone down to pick Dave up from his friend's. I said to Dave did he fancy a walk this afternoon.

So we're not long back from our walk and I can feel my cheeks hot, like there's blood running round my body. My legs shake and ache and my head is light. It was a hard walk – for me. We went down to Whitehead and walked out by the lighthouse, up round the cliff and back again.

The steps that followed the headland right up to the lighthouse just about murdered me and for the first time in ages I felt my heart really beating – forcing blood round my body to feed my muscles. Not palpitating like a rabbit, but thumping like a person. The air was warm with only a light breeze and I had to take my coat and scarf off.

On the walk towards the lighthouse, a robin sat right beside the path singing. It was completely fearless and really going for it. It was so close I could see right into its mouth and its tiny shiny eye. And it sang and sang! It wasn't bothered by us at all. And then on the way back a huge bee landed on Dave's chest and all I could say was there's a bee on you and kind of back away. I thought if I hit it, I might hit it further onto him and then it might sting him. He flicked his T-shirt and it sort of fell-flew off, sleepy and not all there. Kind of like it was lured out of a winter sleep early by the bright warm day.

It was funny the way it happened – the birds and the bees. We decided Dave should have his own TV show called Bewilderness Dave. Friend of the six legged, four legged, two legged and legless.

We surprised ourselves by laughing.

Only when we were on our way back along the path did I start talking about what was going through my head. Maybe it was the extra oxygen, the nearness of the sea or the fantastic sunny day – maybe it was because they were a fitting backdrop for my small, but I suppose momentous decision.

I told him about the letter saying that there was no counselling available at the minute. And I told him about all the sites I'd seen where people talk about their depression going on for months and being so helpless. And I said about the fact that there just seemed to be no help available. You could only get so much help and then... you either go on waiting, and being depressed, or you stop waiting, and think about maybe doing it yourself.

Which meant I had to make the decision. To make myself better. There was only me – no outside help available. No calculators, no translation dictionaries and no reference texts. It would all just have to be in my head.

The depression has been real – but I also have the feeling that I have been punishing myself by feeling this way. And I think it's time to stop punishing me.

By looking for outside help, I've been looking for someone else to stop me beating my own back. To take the big stick off me.

I'm going to stay on the anti-depressants – hopefully they should help me regain my balance, but I really can't expect them to do all the work.

My cheeks are burning and my head is spinning! That's what the planet does for you! That's probably the furthest I've walked in five or six months.

I looked up at the seagulls and felt heavy. I was imprisoned by gravity glue. Walking is a funny thing. It moves your world along from one spot to another, not great distances, and you're always on this world. Gravity glue is a dangerous substance. You could fall off a cliff. But we didn't. We just kept on walking.

I think if you stop long enough, you'll fall off. But momentum juice keeps you going. Momentum juice stops you falling off.

Today there was a song by Soulwax in my head, and I don't know what you call the song but the one line that kept going over in my head was 'Somethin's gotta give, somethin's gotta give, I don't know-oh-ohw'.

When I told Dave what was in my head – and the fact that that song was in my head, I didn't know what it was that was 'going to have to give'.

I think I might be drunk on air. I feel the way you do when you get out of a bath that's too hot or you've just been born out of shell.

Nuts. Lunacy. Pure, 100% natural, organic madness. I was babbling, almost raving. I was that bee, lured out of sleep not by warmth but by impatience and frustration and off-balance brain chemicals. It wasn't the right time. Weeks after serious suicidal thoughts was too early for progress, but I didn't know anything about mental illness, what to expect, how long recovery would take or what truly caused me to collapse. I had no patience with myself and I didn't have it in me to give myself a break. I would simply get better through sheer drive and determination. And with no professional voice to advise me otherwise, I thought all my ravings made perfect sense. Poor, long-suffering Dave.

Recovery DIY

I tried everything the books suggested and more. I read up on aromatherapy and took baths in clouds of sandalwood and went to bed in drifts of lavender. I dropped liquids into my water to help me 'find joy and hope'. I swallowed Omega 3 tablets to improve the health of my brain and burped fish liver all day. I went for a massage in a beautiful salon by the sea and thought about how much I must disgust the girl. I would've been better opening the door, throwing money at her and running away. It would have been less fraught.

None of the 'therapies' worked for me. I found the most comforting and uplifting thing to be sitting with my mother eating Cadbury's Turkish Delight. Sometimes we sat at home, sometimes we parked the car by the sea and watched power walkers storm up and down the promenade while we shared our thick rosy chocolate.

I drifted from day to day, feeling the same, but knowing that I couldn't put off work forever. I couldn't expect them to keep paying my salary and I had no savings to fall back on. My boss felt coming back would be the best thing for me. We met for coffee and she told me there was a project she wanted me to work on, one she thought I'd really enjoy. She wanted me to write and produce a video for a client, and I'd need to travel around the country with a crew and a presenter, interviewing successful businesswomen. It would be good for me, she said. The wife of a friend had had depression once and her doctor advised her to get out into the world as much as possible.

The thought of talking to all those people made me breathless with panic. But maybe getting out and about would help, and I was willing to try anything. Work might be good for me.

I returned to work at the end of February. It was too soon.

Went back to work today and I feel like shite. It was crap and I was straight into the usual shit. A couple of times I felt like crying.

They've started another copywriter – no doubt, he'll do all the fun jobs I enjoy and I'll be stuck with the pitches and big presentations, which stress me out.

I started having bad thoughts on the way home tonight, on the motorway. Just blackness. God, I wish I could.

I have to find some way out of this.

Drudge

My bosses admitted that by having only one copywriter in place, they had left themselves exposed. They'd taken a risk, and they should have managed that risk. However, they were able to recruit quickly – my boss's husband knew someone through his rugby club. I felt like part of a machine that had broken down, a factor to be risk-managed rather than a person who had been ill. To the bosses, it was the book that 'broke' me, therefore, I broke myself. And while that was true to an extent, no one seemed to feel that writing every major pitch and campaign for a couple of years might be rather a lot for one person.

My depression was quickly forgotten, and I was back writing and presenting within a week. With two copywriters in the agency, there was less pressure and I started producing good ideas again, but I was miserable and paranoid. I made the video my boss wanted me to do and I let the director and presenter take the reins. I cringed with fear and discomfort every day of the shoot. Conversation exhausted me and the meds made me sleep so heavily, I kept everyone late each morning when we stayed in a hotel. I lost some shoes and a shirt, and met lots of energetic, happy businesswomen who lived in beautiful homes, had beautiful children and had their shit totally together. I didn't watch the final edit; I didn't care what it was like. The project didn't help me at all. I was still deeply unhappy.

Looking back at diary entries where I describe crying on the way to work, crying in the toilets, and hating myself for not having the guts to throw myself in front of a train, it's pretty obvious that Zispin wasn't the right drug for me. My depression was numbed by Zispin, but there was no lift in mood. Perhaps no drug could have lifted me at the time, but it might have been worth trying others. The misery was relentless, and I know it makes for relentless reading. In March I wrote:

Still here. Still feeling like shit all squared. From things I've read and views of the world in general, things don't get any better. They just go on and on, the same.

I've been going to bed early, sometimes at 8 or 9 o'clock. I'm just sick of myself and can't stand to be inside my own head anymore.

Dave is still working nightshift and he says he'll come off it because I feel this way. But I said he didn't need to. I might still go to bed early, even if he was here. And it's me I'm sick of, not him. His work announced another round of pay offs, so we don't know how stable his job is.

We discussed kids and I suggested we try for a baby when I get off the anti-depressants. Most of the time I feel OK, even though I know life is shit and can only get shitter from here on in. When I think of the future, I can't see joy. I see the death of our parents and then the death of my brother and sisters and then if we have kids, all the dangers they'll face as they're growing up and the things that could happen to them. There must be joy in it, otherwise why would so many people do it?

I know I'm working well but it holds no satisfaction for me. I do it well because I can, not because I should or because I'm working towards anything. I'm not. I got what I wanted. I always thought getting what I wanted would make me happy, but it didn't.

I spent so long working for what I wanted that I can't handle living without aiming for something. I feel like I've lost my goal. I've lost my soul. Part of me is gone. I've lost myself.

I still notice things like birdsong and sunlight. I get ideas for stories, but I have no motivation to write them. I got an invitation to a party at the publisher's. I don't think I can be arsed going.

I don't really care about Fodder *anymore. I have lost hope. Poor* Fodder. *I feel sorry for it. I don't feel sorry for me. I try not to complain because I'm sure Dave and Mummy are tired of me complaining.*

I nearly cried this morning before I went to work and I nearly cried at work. But I held it in. It isn't useful. It has no point. I can't help feeling that nothing has a point anymore. I told Dave that on Friday night. I confessed that I don't see the point of going on and nothing holds any joy for me anymore. I am empty inside. But I just go on, I just carry on with the same routine. I don't know why I do. I just do.

I would like to stop. But I don't.

I go to bed early to escape myself but as sure as shit I will wake up and things will be the same and I will still be here. And I will just go on. I feel like I've been shipwrecked.

Depression makes you incredibly self-absorbed and so I couldn't see how grim it was for Dave to hear that my life – the life I shared with him – was joyless and pointless. In my defence, I did encourage him to go out and see his friends a lot, and was relieved when he went, but it's testament to his great patience and resilience that he stuck by me.

Daily grind

The adrenaline produced in the run-up to pitches made me jumpy and oversensitive, and because pitches are the lifeblood of an agency, paranoia was constant. I felt desolate, but my drive and need for approval wouldn't allow me to take more time off. I continued working, grinding my back teeth while I slept to the point they cracked.

I became convinced my boss was persecuting me. I recorded everything she said in my journal, studying it from every angle, picking it apart, believing she was trying to drive me out of the agency or back to madness. Most of it can be put down to my own paranoia, but it's clear she had no understanding of depressive illness and the fact that it can go on for months, sometimes years. I think she found me moody, recalcitrant, stubborn and miserable. And that would piss anyone off.

Eleven months after my initial breakdown, I told her I had an appointment with a Community Psychiatric Nurse (CPN) and would need to leave the office. She looked at me in confusion – who, what, why? She had forgotten that I had ever been depressed, or that I might still be. And I thought that because I was no longer at breakdown point, that I was probably well again.

Re-reading the wretched, self-damning journal entries, it's evident the depression had not lifted. I thought that hating everything about myself, believing I was repugnant and understanding why everyone else would hate me and treat me like shit, was quite normal.

The CPN listened. And listened. And listened. I was relieved to have someone to whom I could offload all my angst. And boy, did I offload. I seemed to ramble on for hours. She was patient and astute, and gave me tips on improving how I felt about myself, trying to help me get more perspective on my 'failure'. Either I wasn't ready to hear it or she didn't have what I needed. The appointments went on for six weeks and then it was over. My psychiatric care was done. I continued with Zispin, but I felt like a castaway.

I grew resentful at work. While I knew advertising was a business and I was a resource, at the same time, I was hurt when I wrote the tender and creative campaign that won the agency an extremely valuable account and received a bottle of champagne for my efforts, as did every other person in the agency, including people who didn't work on the pitch. 'Failure is not an option, Tara,' I had been told as I wrote the tender proposal. I wasn't their superstar anymore. I was damaged goods. I had put on weight, my clothes were too tight, my skin was dull, my hair neglected, and I looked stressed and exhausted. I disgusted myself. I wasn't very agency at all.

In my journal I talked about how much I envied colleagues who moved on to other jobs and I'm impressed by my own tenacity. That bottle of champagne stayed on my desk until I left the agency a year later. I don't know where it went after that.

Tara West

After

Tara West

Frabjous day

My mood picked up as soon as I made the decision to leave. I had something to aim for and I planned to do freelance work and balance it with my own writing. I recorded in my journal how moody Dave seemed at times, and with hindsight, I don't know how he survived all this without succumbing to depression himself. I made life very tough for him. He was concerned about our finances, but he knew how unhappy I was at work and we both hoped self-employment would be different. I said I could always go back to an agency if we needed a more secure income.

I gave three months' notice to allow them time to find another experienced copywriter. They recruited immediately, but the new copywriter had her own ways and the agency was used to mine. Within months the bosses were giving the work back to me. The time apart improved our relationship and my boss even said that if the freelancing didn't work out, she hoped I would come back.

I paid myself a pittance of a wage every month, enough to cover my contribution to the mortgage and bills. There was no money for treats or bras, but I gave myself 'pocket money' so I could meet friends for lunch and coffee. I created radio scripts, press copy and other documents, and freed from the stress of pitching, early rising and old pressures, my mood continued to improve. There were still ups and downs, but there were days when I began to recognise myself – a less fearful, more balanced, more grown-up me. The depression had lasted around two years, but it wasn't the passing of time that had made me more grown-up. It was having suicidal thoughts and coming out the other side. It was looking back and being able to see myself and others as deserving of sympathy. I know it's a cliché, but the experience had given me much more perspective.

New life

Seven months into my freelance career, my mother and I stood outside the Royal Maternity Hospital in steely January sunlight and stared at an ultrasound scan. There were two babies inside me. Two! Dave couldn't get away from work so my mother came with me to have early scans. I'd had some bleeding and we thought I might be miscarrying. But no. There were two little blobs inside me, two clear heartbeats.

I rang Dave. We were giddy with joy and excitement. How could he be a dad? How could I be a mother? Shiiiiiiiiiiiit. We were in our mid-thirties, but we were still kids ourselves, listening to loud music, playing video games and watching sci-fi – doing the things we used to do before my breakdown.

I wasn't worried though – I had my own mother to show me. I didn't know how to hold or bathe or feed or comfort a baby; I hadn't even changed a nappy before. I never babysat for other families. I never really liked babies, they were whiny, needy and greedy. But she loved them all, and she regularly looked after and indulged my brother's and sisters' children. She was a loving mother, but a magical grandmother, full of imagination and fun and giving out sweets when no one was looking. I couldn't wait for my children to meet her.

She was as excited about the pregnancy as we were. She began knitting and she was not a champion knitter. She embarked upon the creation of a big soft white blanketty kind of thing, which lay on her bosom as she nodded off, her glasses perched on the end of her nose.

We spent more time together now that I was freelance. She was silly and fun, and as she aged, she seemed to lose much of the anxiety and self-consciousness that my grandmother had helped create in her. When she was with me, she was self-assured and cared less what people thought. I have a photograph of her from that time, holding up two liquorice allsorts in front of her eyes. It was hard not to want to spend time with her: she would say and do outrageously funny things just to make me laugh.

She would duck and hide from me in supermarkets, buy coconuts as presents and wear frozen peas on her knees on hot days. When I visited her in the new flat she and her partner had moved to, she would shout, 'Love you... love you... love you!' down the lift shaft as I descended, changing the pitch to create her own Doppler effect. We still went shopping on Saturdays and she would stand in the downstairs hallway of the flats watching and waiting for me to pick her up. I would drive past the door, turn the car and come back so I was pointing the right way. Each time, when I pulled up, she would be at the window faux-sobbing, as if she were a child whose spirits soared when she saw me, then crashed when I drove past.

I asked her why she never kept a journal and she said that she did once, when she was still married to my father, but it was all in tiny shorthand and the only word she could make out was 'bastard'. She said she wouldn't start a new journal because the only thing it would say would be 'fuck fuck fuck fuck fuck bastard fuck'. She still didn't know how to express her anger; she didn't really know how to express anything with her partner. With him, she was compliant and passive and I put it down to the need for approval that was instilled in her as a child. That, and possibly a fear of being alone again. Without protest or complaint, she accepted his demands for freshly ironed shirts, despite hating ironing and all other housework. She made the bland, garlic-free food he liked, even though she despised cooking and found their meals profoundly boring. She loved the food I made, loaded with garlic and spices, but she couldn't bring anything like that into the flat: her partner couldn't stand the smell. I was careful not to criticise him or the relationship in front of her, although I'm sure my feelings must have leaked out sometimes. I found it difficult leaving her home to the flat when I knew she was going inside to be someone else entirely.

I told myself I should be writing the next book, not playing daft games with my mother. Friends and colleagues kept asking when they could expect to see the next novel, and I was playing hooky. I'd planned to start writing again once I went freelance, but my energy was still low and it just wasn't fun anymore. Coming up with ideas was a slog; I was forcing the writing and it felt like hard work. My efforts petered off until I stopped altogether. I didn't forget about writing though. I regularly beat myself up for not putting the effort in and not following through on my early promise.

I was having fun with my mother. She gave me a book with prayers and poems from different religions and non-religions from around the world, we listened to seventeenth century choral music in my house, we wrote each other letters while sitting together, and she called us 'ineffectuals'. When I parked illegally to run into a shop, she would close her eyes in the front seat and pretend to be dead, just in case traffic wardens approached. Sometimes she would put Classic FM on in the car so we could stare out the window and the old women, limping dogs and skipping children would seem dramatic and portentous. We called it 'watching the human tragedy unfold'. She was hilarious and joyous and turned things round for me without even knowing.

My pregnancy heralded the realisation of our dream list. Dave and I had the house (not double-fronted, but still nice); we didn't have pots of money, but we were doing OK, and children were finally on their way. I imagined they would look Scandinavian like Dave, with his golden skin and hair, but have the long legs that run in my family (sorry). But the next time I went for a scan, there was only one baby. The other had disappeared. It happens sometimes – the weaker twin dies and is 'reabsorbed'. I don't know where he or she went. I feel that it was a boy, but of course, I can't know that. He would have been Oscar. I still think about him.

I continued to work as the baby grew, and received an offer of a full-time job at another agency. It made sense to go back to full-time work. I was feeling a bit better, I wasn't writing the next book anyway, and when the baby came, I would need more security. I didn't want her – I knew it was a her – to grow up in poverty or even at the risk of poverty. I decided I wouldn't go back to work until after the baby was born and I'd had six months' maternity leave. That, I knew, would be a magical time. Me, Dave, my mother, my baby, together for six months. She would show us how to really love a child.

She's still here

I was seven and half months into the pregnancy before I began to look pregnant. As the weeks went on, I suffered from fluid retention, and the bigger I got, the harder it was to lug my swollen legs and feet around. While my baby grew, my mother faced health problems. She had several defibrillation treatments to try to settle an irregular heartbeat, her blood pressure was difficult to control, and she was hospitalised for seven weeks to fight an infection in her heart.

Hospital visiting times were limited and it irritated me that other patients wanted to talk to her when I was there. They slept in beds beside her and could talk to her all day long, I only had her for an hour or so in the afternoon or evening. Although she was responding to treatment, her illness made me panicky and I wanted to make the most of every minute spent with her. We discussed names for the baby and how she hoped I would name it after her, but not actually use any of her names, which narrowed the options a little. We giggled over the other patients: a woman who thought she was praying in the direction of the hospital church, but it turned out to be the canteen, and a man who was playing with the controls on his bed and got stuck five feet in the air.

She told me that she had had time to think about things in hospital and from now on she was going to be different. She and her partner had been together for almost twenty years and they never got married. She would have liked to, but he didn't ask and, of course, she didn't bring it up. From now on, she said, she was going to focus more on herself and less on keeping him in stew and ironed shirts. She was going to eat garlic and go on trips and spend her money on herself.

She was going to 'outlive him', she said, because only then would she be free to be who she really was – the person she was when she was with me. It had been a long, slow journey for her, accepting herself as she really was, and even if it was only for a few hours on a Saturday afternoon, she still got there in the end.

Within two weeks of leaving hospital, she was rushed back into the intensive care unit. She had picked up 'superbug' infections while she was being treated for the infection in her heart. She was in the ICU for nine days, sedated, while machines fed her oxygen, fluids and drugs. We visited regularly – my brother, sisters, their partners, children, Dave and I – sitting by her bedside, staring at her still face and closed eyes, holding her swollen yellowish hands. Did she know we were there? There was no reaction, just occasional low bleeps from the monitors and rattles and gasps from the ventilator.

One Thursday afternoon I parked at the hospital and found her partner waiting in the long dim corridor outside the closed doors of the ICU. She'd had diarrhea and they were changing her bed. Her internal organs were failing.

He turned to me, crying. 'I thought she couldn't love me because I couldn't be a man for her. It's the tablets I'm on,' he said.

I was confused. I thought he was going to tell me something about her, but this was... I was stunned.

Looking back, I think he was having regrets, as people do when their loved ones are dying. He had detected my mother's frustration over the years, but he had mistaken it for something else. He was as desperate and lost as I was. I put on a surreally sympathetic face until the nurse opened the door and let us in.

We washed our hands at the little sink and sat on the bench beside my mother's bed, the machines doing their quiet work. Did she know we were there? There was no indication that she did. Strangely, her eyes were watering. My mother's partner asked the nurse why.

'It's just a reaction,' she said, scuttling briskly across the room.

I didn't know what that meant. But I've always wondered was it something else. Did my mother know we were there? Did she know what was coming?

I leaned close and told her that we'd decided on a name for the baby and I would tell her when she got out of the ICU. Her partner sat beside me, wiping his face with his handkerchief.

Later, at home, as I lay on our bed and read, I heard myself whimper. I sat up and looked at Dave.

The phone rang. My nephew told me to come to the hospital now. I could hear my sisters in the background.

There was a hole in the universe, in me. We were upside down. Something had been torn out of me, off me, a physical thing.

We were crammed into a room beside the ICU with my brother and sisters and their families.

Her partner was on the phone to someone. 'Joan's dead,' he said.

Dead.

The word was a mallet. Without substance, but with the power to take away my breath and flatten me.

And inside, my baby, kicking because she was struggling. Breathe, breathe. She'll be here soon.

The book of prayers and poems said she was gone, but she was only in the next room. In my father's mansion, there are many rooms. Not gone. Still here.

We suffer. We suffer.

Helpless

Farha Daisy West arrived on the 12th September 2005 at 11am. Farha is an Arabic name and it means happiness. Daisy is short for Marguerite Daisy, after my mother whose full name was Margaret Joan, but she never liked Margaret or Joan, and we figured Daisy could be a connection to her, albeit a nebulous one. West is Dave's name, the one I took when I married him. It's not my original name, but then I'm not who I was.

In the photographs, the newborn has been placed on my breast and I look down at her, my face arranged into an expression of compassion, but if I'm honest, I was horrified. I'd just been through a thirty-hour labour at the end of which a baby was vacuumed out of me, a student sewed up my rips and they handed me a thing that looked like a big slab of liver.

She cried constantly in the maternity ward. A nurse took her away on the second night to see if she could settle her, but handed her back an hour later, still wailing. When the obstetrician did his rounds, I couldn't remember my baby's name or whether I'd had a girl or a boy. I vomited everything I ate and was so sleep-deprived, I saw faces coming out of the wall.

Families gathered round the newborns, and mothers and grandmothers settled the babies. My family and friends came to visit and assumed I would, could, settle Farha. I couldn't. I didn't know what I was doing. I was frantic. None of the other mothers seemed as anxious as I was. And the more stressed I became, the more fretful and unhappy and screamy Farha grew. The only thing that settled her was being stuck to my breast, even if she wasn't feeding. Dave's friend bought a dummy in the hospital shop and we plugged it in to see what would happen.

I have a photograph of a brand new Farha, tiny and formless in her giant sleepsuit, her purple face almost completely obscured by a pink dummy. It worked. Sucking and sucking and sucking noisily, she could finally settle while not glued to me. Her eyes, already wide open and focused, were staring straight into mine. And when she wasn't looking into my eyes, she was looking for them. Only I would satisfy her.

I knew a baby would be a lot of work but this sent shockwaves to my core. I dropped lamb dhansak and saag aloo all over her as I ate, trying to fill up what she was sucking out of me. I found breastfeeding very painful, but all new mothers were urged to do it, and with the health visitor's encouragement I persevered. I ran out of milk, leaving Farha and me very upset. I was a poor mother in every sense. When I did have milk, I was passing my own adrenaline straight into her system.

No health professionals deduced that I might need help, even though I had been treated for severe depression and my mother had just died. Of course, I filled in the questionnaires to ascertain whether I had post-natal depression and dodged the issue quite smartly, which is easy for any intelligent woman who's completely doolally.

Did I ever think about harming myself? Piss off. And have my baby taken away from me? Think I'll tick the no box, even though I've hit my head off the wall hard enough to see stars. Do I feel despair? My mother died of hospital-acquired infections just a short time ago and all the things we were going to do together died with her. I can't go out because I can't leave this room. Tick no.

Dave was exhausted and whereas death, birth and sleeplessness left me lost and desperate, they made him angry. He battled through his parental duties in silent, seething resignation and all conversation dried up. He took Farha on long drives along the coast to settle her and let me sleep, but I couldn't switch off. I was worried he would strangle or smother her. My mind was in freefall. There were no rules or precedents where my head was at.

This didn't feel like the depression I'd had before, and I didn't recognise it. I thought it was grief for my mother. I felt like I was walking along the edge of an endless cliff and I knew I couldn't fall off because I was holding a baby and I wouldn't let any harm come to her, yet the fear and danger were always there. It was, Dave agrees, a very tough time.

At three weeks, Farha started to smile, and at eight weeks, her sunny, curious personality started to show through. I wheeled her buggy for miles and miles every day, filling in time until I went back to work. I couldn't do this parenting thing, it was awful. When I handed her across to my sister, even for a few minutes, the relief I felt was enormous. And yet I loved Farha so much, I was stripped raw by guilt.

I believed that my baby was disadvantaged having me for a mother and I felt the most searing pity for her. Panic and dread followed me everywhere. I'm doing this all wrong, I thought. I will mess this up, I will mess her up. God, please, if you're there, help her. I missed my own mother and the comfort and advice she would have provided. But even in my desperation, the old drive kicked in: I would try to get this right. I would work at it. I wouldn't let Farha down. I gathered books and read up on how to be a mother.

OK, so, first thing, get a routine started. But stay flexible. Anticipate your baby's needs and you'll avoid a lot of screaming – get her into bed before the third yawn, have the bottles ready, line up toys and interesting things for when she's likely to get bored. Don't play with her when you feed her at night, just do the feed, cuddle her and put her down (and still those eyes, shining in the dark, staring into mine). Swaddle her, rock her, pat her, sing. For her, that's like being back in the womb. Play with her, talk to her, read to her. Respect her and who she is, she is a person after all. She will do the same for you.

Dave, Farha and I established daily rituals and good habits, which helped forestall and dissipate the screaminess. We coped, but stress combined with grief and sleeplessness turned me into a sad ghost living on the other side of the looking glass, and Dave into an angry satellite, part of us, but no longer central. Our relationship was suffering, and we barely spoke.

My sister, a long-time childminder, agreed to look after Farha during the day and I looked forward to going back to work. Not because I loved my job, but because I wanted to escape the desperation and sadness of maternity leave. I grinned and waved like mad when I drove away so that Farha would feel confident and happy when I was gone. I missed my gorgeous, curious, delightful baby, and loved the smell of her on my hands, but going back to work was a relief.

Going pro

After maternity leave, I worked in an agency with a cerebral MD who'd been trained to international standards, worked on international brands and expected the same professional practice of everyone. There were no more expensive gifts and charisma-led pitches; there were endless taxing debates, robust research, facts, insights and a smart new vocabulary. We used 'proven processes that utilised proprietary tools and led to sound business decisions and effective campaigns'.

It was what I'd been doing for years, but I didn't know it was a 'process'. I didn't use 'tools' and I clearly didn't know the industry argot. I just read stuff, thought about what motivated people and wrote something I thought would have an impact based on what I knew. And it worked. I shared some of my previous tender proposals with the MD and he was impressed by the fact that I did it all intuitively. I was offended and pleased at the same time.

A second copywriter did all the pitching and I was happy to sit back and let him bask in the stress. I couldn't do it again. I was mediocre at best. Everyone knew that. My mediocrity aside, I had a very young baby and I was numb with sleep deprivation. I didn't know where I'd parked the car and was washing my face with a baby wipe every morning. I wasn't up for more challenges. I had a decent salary and was providing daily

149

copywriting support, which meant coming up with ideas, writing scripts, creating radio ads, writing press and long copy, and avoiding responsibility wherever possible.

I felt there was nothing for it but to accept working life and quit trying to be a writer or artist, or whatever the younger me had ever believed in. I didn't have the time or energy to write, what with working all day and spending my evenings feeding and bathing Farha, reading to her, putting her to bed, and preparing bottles, food, clothes, toys and bags for the next day. I assumed I had to do everything for her. I had to do it all and get it right. Unfairly, Dave was excluded, and I drooped and shook with fatigue.

And yet, writing kept coming back into my head. I would see news or reviews of new work by my writing contemporaries and I would be angry to the point of wanting to throw the newspaper or kick the computer. It wasn't the poor old writers I was angry at, it was me. I'd fucked up my writing career. It was three years since the book had been published, invitations to readings and festivals had long dried up, everyone had forgotten about it and I probably didn't even know *how* to write these days. Even if Farha did become more settled and I had more time in the evenings, I couldn't write and work like I did last time, it nearly killed me. I would have to make a choice, and if that were so, then writing was over. I had a child to support. Advertising was it.

And yet.

Writing would not die. It just hung around at the back of my mind, nagging at me and annoying me. Writing was a zombie who would not piss off back to its neat earthy plot in the boneyard. It hung around, stinking up the place. It wanted my brain.

I pretended it wasn't there. Farha started sleeping through the night and Dave and I were getting on better, we talked more, and one of the things we talked about was moving house. James was still our neighbour, but we had a new neighbour on the other side, who mounted a huge union flag above his front door as soon as he moved in. To some people, the union flag is a symbol of identity. To us, having lived in an estate where it was flown above or wrapped around parading drunks, it was an indicator of loutish behaviour and the potential for violence. I worried that I, the mental magnet, had somehow drawn him there and I didn't want Farha to grow up in that. It was time to move.

I embraced the life of a suburban professional and everything that came with it, including the biggest mortgage Dave and I could afford. The double-fronted house we found was in a quiet street about eight miles from Belfast and ten minutes from Carrickfergus. It had gardens front and rear, a garage, and when I went to view it on my way home from work, Dave was already there, standing in the doorway, holding Farha and waving. It looked like they already lived there. Someone somewhere was cooking something garlicky, kids were tossing a rugby ball and little girls were playing with a skipping rope – a skipping rope!

This was the house. We might live on pasta and salad cream for the foreseeable future, but this was the house.

Dave organised the move on a seriously tight budget. He found the cheapest van rental in Belfast and roped in mates to help lug furniture in and out of houses. I shuttled up and down the road with my car full of plates, utensils, pictures, mirrors, toys, clothes and all the things we'd gathered up over the years. It probably looked like Steptoe and Son were moving in, but we didn't care. We were starting a new life.

Working moves

There was a turnover of staff. Old faces left, new faces joined, new faces left, and the creative team shrank. I was the only copywriter again. The MD needed someone to head up the creative team and asked if I would be interested. I thought he must be desperate if he was asking me.

His new processes formalised and gave structure to my own thinking and I 'utilised' them often, but I was second-rate. And clearly not right in the head. Surely he could hear how inarticulate, shaky and anxious I was. He was smart, he must know how beat up I was on the inside. He said I was head and shoulders above the rest of the creative team and the strongest conceptual thinker in Belfast. He was blowing smoke up my ass. I told him I didn't want to be the creative lead.

When the previous Creative Director left and I turned down the role, the MD recruited a new Deputy Creative Director, Anna, who would be appointed to the Creative Director role if, after a six month trial period, she proved she was right for the job. Anna was a fresh-faced, blonde Austrian woman with square white teeth and buckets of energy. She had an exotic accent, a wide smile and wore her tight jeans tucked into her high-heeled boots, just like my mother had. She adopted one of the meeting rooms as her office and spent a lot of time speaking German on the phone. I didn't know who she was talking to or what she was working on, but she certainly looked very busy. She would often come out of her office to chat with me about her travels, her work in other countries and her Irish boyfriend. She said she had to call her bank a lot. She was bankrupt.

One morning she brought me fragrant hawthorn flowers she had picked on her walk to work. I thanked her for them – it was a lovely gesture – but it unsettled me. My mother told me not to bring hawthorn indoors, it's bad luck. I was uncomfortable with it and, later, took it back outside.

Because I liked her and was impressed by her exotic background, stories and energy, it took a few weeks for me to realise what was going on. As my superior, she made the decisions and she decided that I should do all the work and she would march up and down the corridor looking enthusiastic about it.

We needed ideas for a new creative brief, and we had one day to turn them around. I was surprised she had no ideas, but maybe she was just busy with other stuff. On another project, she shortlisted ideas that seemed off-brief to me. Another day, we had to make an animated storyboard to show what a TV ad would look like for a new dessert product. I booked time in the recording studio, Anna booked time in the edit studio, and we went to brief the editor together. When it came to putting the animated storyboard together, I suddenly found I had seven radio commercials to record all at the same time and wasn't available to help her, but I was sure Anna would be fine on her own.

I admit it – I set her up. I deliberately left her to work alone. I needed proof she could do the job without me and that I wasn't just being paranoid. It turned out that I wasn't the only one to notice Anna wasn't all she first appeared: designers and art directors complained they couldn't respect someone who had no talent and account managers said clients laughed at her. She didn't survive the six months' trial period. What this unpleasant little episode proved to me was that I was capable of taking on a more senior role. I had been doing Anna's job for her.

I agreed to take on the Deputy Creative Director role, with a view to becoming Creative Director. There would be more money in it and that was a relief, but part of me suspected it was a mistake. I couldn't do this job. I just wasn't good enough. I would need an escape.

The writing zombie lurched awake.

A happier place

The difficult and exhausting newborn had turned into a curious, busy toddler. Farha was becoming more independent without going through the tantrum stage. She was beginning to talk, bellowing out single words and demands, and messy play was her favourite pastime. I liked to see her covered in spaghetti in the kitchen or toddling through mud and puddles. I wanted her to learn that exploring and having fun is much better than getting it right or being perfect. She was always an outdoorsy child, at one point venturing outside on Christmas Day in just a pair of pants. She was not overly affectionate, so on the rare occasions she did give out hugs, we knew she really meant them.

I had been back at work for almost two years and was commuting by train. It gave me time to read or stare into space and it helped keep the daily routine in place – as long as the train was on time. One night, there was a problem with signals, and I would be stuck at the station for fifty minutes. I called Dave to let him know, then watched the stranded passengers filling in time. Some played on phones, some read, some caught up on sleep, others twiddled thumbs. I had no book and I didn't have enough cash to buy one. Damn it, there was nothing for it. I would have to amuse myself.

I started scribbling in the back pages of my diary as the writing zombie sat down beside me.

The zombie was coming to life on the page: she had been a girl, a woman, once, but a devastating experience concerning poets had scarred her so deeply, she now had a debilitating fear of poetry. And poets. Because that was silly and funny and, well, like me and that BBC Radio 3 thing. She suffered from depression and had been living quietly for a long time, avoiding stress and upset, but hers was a half-life, caught between life and death, cold and without love. Now she was waking up, her winter was coming to an end.

Could I write fiction about depression? Well, Sylvia Plath had, sort of, and that was a fairly depressing book. Could I make it funny? Because, if I was going to do this – the writing zombie was not going to leave me alone – then I might as well make it fun, and a bit of challenge. I would make this book dark. And funny at the same time.

I was excited to be writing again, making notes when I had time during the day and writing in the evening after Farha went to bed, but progress was frustratingly slow. Work was busy, I had more responsibility and I was tired in the evenings. It took over a year to write just five chapters and it had been a long time since the first novel. I was impatient for progress. I knew that the Arts Council of Northern Ireland provided support for writers to create new work, so I got online and read up on the process.

Well, I knew all about 'process'; I'd been following processes and writing about them in tender proposals for years. I downloaded the application pack and filled in the forms, using all the experience I'd gained at work. I provided evidence of my commitment to writing (one published novel and a list of festivals I'd read at), my potential to develop as an artist (five chapters of a new novel, plus synopsis, plus list of areas I wanted to improve in as a writer) and a budget plan (the i's thoroughly investigated, the t's clearly costed up) all in support of my overall aim of taking unpaid leave from my job in order to complete my second novel. I thought through every angle, imagined every question they might ask, and spent weeks refining, editing and shaping the submission.

I hadn't mentioned any of this to the MD, but then I never really believed my application would be successful.

They awarded me the maximum available to individuals and invited me up for a chat.

Reviewing the past

Damian, the Literature Officer at the Arts Council, wore a quality suit, had a shaved head and small, intense eyes. His clothes said professional public servant, but his demeanour said poet. I didn't hold that against him, though. Rather, I liked him. An assistant wheeled a tray of tea and coffee into his book-lined office and he poured us some tea.

He was one of the brightest people I had ever met, and he talked in long sentences that weaved together four or five different concepts. I found I had to list them all in my head so that I could converse in return. He said he was a big fan of *Fodder* and I thought he was mad. Mistaken, misguided. I truly thought he was pissing about. But then he said,

'I remember the reviews. It had a big impact. The critical reception was excellent, wasn't it?'

'Was it?'

He looked at me in confusion, then carried on in his winding sentences, smiling, then serious, then smiling, because he was pleased I was writing again.

That night I went home and dug out the box where I kept the cuttings from the publication of *Fodder*. I pulled out the reviews... and the reviews were... well, they weren't anywhere near as bad as I remembered. There was certainly valid criticism – Cookie's voice wasn't always convincing, the structure was messy at times –

but most of it was approving. Some of it was very supportive.

They were all wrong. They had jumped on the bandwagon. They felt sorry for me and were being nice. The book was awful and I hated it. The box was full of posters, flyers, articles and interviews, reminders of how terrible the book was despite what they all said. I shut everything back inside and heaved it into the loft where I didn't have to look at it.

I took the unpaid leave from work and found some rented office space: a tiny little room in the shadow of capacious Victorian redbrick houses near Queen's University. Every day I listened to a melancholy, poignant and yearning playlist on the train, setting the tone for the book. I picked up a coffee and wore a backpack with my cobwebby old laptop inside, the one Dave had bought me eight years before. I had no internet in my office; it was just me, my desk, my giant stained thesaurus and my dear little zombie friend. What a magical summer we had together as seagulls wheeled fretfully over their chimney nests and huge bees sheltered from sharp sun showers on my windowsill. I blasted through the writing, living so deeply in my fictional world that I achieved some kind of zen-like state. My purpose and focus were clear, the story flowed and my body regulated itself like never before. At home, Farha was learning to ride a bike without stabilisers and had made her first best friend.

Dave was rebuilding an old Vespa he had found rotting in someone's garage. We were busy doing what we loved, and we were happy.

But the little zombie and I had to come back down to earth sometime. I remember glassy shafts of light crossing my desk in the evening of my last day in the rented office. The summer was over and the first draft was done. I had missed the last train, so I called a taxi and went home. I still miss that little office.

Moody mummy

I continued to work on the book when I returned to my job, refining and editing and shaping the words after Farha went to bed. I handed the manuscript to my agent in December and he believed he would find a publisher within weeks. But weeks went by and nothing happened. No publishers were interested. They thought it was insightful, compassionate, funny, but it just wasn't right for them. Over and over again. Not right for them – though they were sure it would find a home somewhere.

Gradually, I began to realise that the book was shit. No one would ever publish it. I was deluded. I was an advertising writer, not a real writer, and I was an idiot to think I could ever be published again. The first one was a fluke.

I grew slow and sluggish, paranoid and frustrated. I felt doomed and hated everything and everyone. I threw my watch in the drawer because it reminded me I was a slave to the machine. I spent my lunchtimes walking and avoiding workmates who might want to chat. Getting up in the morning was desperately hard and I couldn't wait to return to bed every night. I was angry all the time and I explained to Farha,

'Mummy just gets moody sometimes. It's not you. It's not you.'

I couldn't do this to her.

I went back to Dr Corr and she prescribed Sertraline and referred me to a Community

Psychiatric Nurse to be assessed for Cognitive Behavioural Therapy. She thought I would be a good candidate.

I didn't explicitly tell Dave what was going on, rather I casually slipped it into the conversation when we were making dinner and talking about something else. I had stopped telling him when I was feeling down, but of course, he knew me. He knew when something wasn't right. He stared at me ruefully, but didn't pursue it. I didn't want to talk about it. I was afraid – for him, Farha and myself, and I didn't want him to feel my fear. But that meant shutting him out and leaving him to worry alone.

Two weeks after starting Sertraline, I felt a sudden lift, as though in my head I was standing on a kind of platform. It was the strangest feeling, like I had a splint inside my mind that held my mood firmly in place. My energy returned and I felt enthused and excited, so much so that I signed up to do a Masters Degree in Creative Writing, applied for more support from the Arts Council and told the MD I should be Creative Director. Like, right now.

While a mild manic high can be enjoyable, it's never the most practical. Making up for lost time, I completely overcommitted.

Tara West

Learning how to think

Tara West

Nutsville is just a drive away

I have a map to tell me how to get to Holywell. It's a hospital I know from my childhood, but only because neighbours would toss the word around when they were referring to schizos and weirdos and people who were 'terrible bad with their nerves'. To me, as a child, it wasn't a hospital so much as a general impression of hopelessness and things people didn't want to talk about. I suspect most people still have the same impression. I am on my way there.

I rattle up the M2 in my car, late, with the map on the seat beside me. It's September and still warm, and I put the windows down to let in some air, and to make sure the car doesn't smell of smoke, because I need one. I light my cigarette and the wind sucks the map out of the car. I can see it in the mirror, whipping up over the lanes, off to live its own life now. I don't know where I'm going. I'll have to use the Force.

Junction what? Junction Seven. Or is it Six? No, after Junction Six, which is the one for Antrim Area Hospital. So it's Junction Seven. Or is it Six? I sail by Junction Six and swing off at Junction Seven onto a country road. A giant wind turbine swooshes over the modern buildings of Antrim Hospital behind me on the left, and the surrounding land is lush and green, dotted with mature trees. Maybe these fields belonged to a big country house or something.

I keep driving, following the signs for Antrim town. I can't find Holywell Hospital, I'm going to get stuck in Antrim's busy streets, I'm going to be late. Finally, I see a sign for the hospital. I follow it and there it is. So many trees, it's surprisingly pretty here. I stop to look at a map by the main entrance. I can't remember what department I'm looking for. Psychology something. The whole place is psychology something. I remember that the department I'm looking for is near the entrance, so I drive on, peering at the buildings just inside the grounds.

The main buildings are red brick, old, with intricate design details. This is, I realise, a Victorian lunatic asylum and it's beautiful. There are tall waving trees and mature gardens round the edges. I lean this way and that looking for signs, squeezing past delivery vehicles and other cars. Before I know it, I've driven through the entire hospital grounds and popped out the other side. I have one minute to reach the place. I do a lap and end up back where I started. And there it is! It isn't in the grounds, it's just outside, next to the main entrance. On the periphery of Holywell, not inside. So I'm not completely mad, I'm just on the edge of madness. That sounds about right.

I pull in and park on crunching gravel beneath towering sequoia. The air is damp and fresh and it's so quiet I can hear leaves rustling. The Department of Psychological Therapies is based in a house built in the sixties or seventies, now converted into offices and surgeries. I buzz the front door and am admitted remotely. I take a seat in a narrow, empty hallway beside some stairs with a heavy 1960s-looking handrail. It's warm and silent. I wonder who built this house, who lived here, so close to all the nutjobs.

A small woman opens a glass door and asks if I'm Tara. She has tight dark curls, a little round face and bright crinkly eyes. She's the same age as some of my friends. She smiles and shakes my hand. 'I'm Diane. Come on in.'

I follow her into an office where everything seems petite, just like her. I'm tallish and I feel like a prize bull standing in here. It's a relief to sit in the armchair she offers. I don't feel so outlandishly big when she sits down too.

I don't know what to expect. I wonder if I smell of smoke. I look OK, I think. A bit heavy these days, but I haven't been able to manage my weight so well after Zispin. I look professional and together and she maybe wonders what I'm doing here. God knows what kind of people she has to treat – people in the direst need, people in grief, people in poverty. Hope I'm not wasting her time.

I look round the office as she pulls together some papers. There's a whiteboard on the wall and a magnet on the filing cabinet with a picture of a smiling 1950s man with Brilliantined hair saying, 'Therapy has taught me that it's all your fault.' The window overlooks a back garden with a lawn, trees and bushes, and beyond that, fields. Maybe this room was a bedroom or a study at one time. It's quiet. Comfortable and professional at the same time. I can hear my nose whistling.

'OK. First thing I want you to do,' Diane says, handing me some sheets of paper, 'is work through these. These just let me know where you are at the minute.'

'OK.'

'Would you like tea or coffee?'

'Are you having one?'

'I'm not sure if we have any milk. Tea or coffee, how do you like it?'

'Tea. Just milk. I'll have one if you're having one.'

'Won't be a minute. Here's a pen.' She smiles and nips out, and I work through the sheets.

There are three sheets with about twenty questions per side and lots of boxes to tick. They're the same questions I'm used to, but they're more detailed, more nuanced. Some seem irrelevant, even patronising, but I answer as truthfully as I can. It takes me ages because I need to think about the answers.

I compare everything to the tormented days when I wanted to switch myself off and I'm not sure that's right. Depression of yesteryear? Depression of yesterweek? Or depression of today? I feel OK today, but then I'm taking Sertraline.

It's been ten years since my breakdown, and seven years since my mother died. Farha is growing; she is noisy, messy and sensitive, and she glows with energy and life. She knocks my socks off every second of the day. I've been back at work a long time – I'm Head of Creative

Development now – and my moods are up and down. No world-beating highs, but I'm always anxious and the depression keeps coming back. Some days I have very dark thoughts. Most of the time, I don't.

Diane opens the door carrying a mug of tea. 'How're you getting on?'

'Still ticking.' Most people must be quicker than I am. I'm so slow. This is eating into our time together. I'm sure I must be holding her up.

'Take your time.' She sets down the tea and disappears. I realise that I get tea because I'm the patient. This is not a business meeting or a chat between chums, we're here to sort out my thinker. She won't be having tea.

Finally, I finish ticking and Diane sits in the armchair opposite, smiling warmly. These are professional armchairs. Not easy chairs. They have soft seats but hard arms. Don't get too comfortable, they say, we have work to do. And we do.

Diane begins by explaining what Cognitive Behavioural Therapy is and how it works. It's a talking therapy that explores how your thinking influences how you feel and how you act. The way you think is based on core beliefs you hold about yourself, and these beliefs are generally opinions you formed of yourself at a young age. CBT helps you identify these generally flawed core beliefs and recognise when you're having thoughts based on them. Then you reset your thinking based on facts, not your old beliefs. You practise this 'resetting' every day until you do it naturally. It has a high success rate.

I write it all down. I get it.

Actually, I don't. The theory seems sound, but I don't yet understand the impact this will have on me.

We talk through my experiences over the years – the downs, and the one noticeable, glorious up. Diane asks if I've been to see a psychiatrist. She wonders if I might be bipolar. I say no, I haven't, and, no, I don't think so. No cutting off of ears, etc. But then, I'm no expert.

She makes notes, as do I. I'm not just a good candidate for this kind of therapy, I'm perfect: goal-oriented and practical. I bring my own notebook, I buy the textbook and I want to do my homework. More than anything, I want this to work. My biggest worry is that my depression will mess up my daughter for life.

Not good enough

The MD allows me to leave early for my appointment with Diane every second Thursday at 4pm. While he's sympathetic, he admits that my moods make me inconsistent and unpredictable and difficult to manage. He says he hopes this works out for me.

Each appointment begins with my ticking through the boxes on the sheets, which allows Diane to chart my progress over time.

It's misty and damp outside the window and the trees have lost most of their leaves. For my homework, I've had to write down a recent occasion when I experienced a dark mood and identify exactly what I was thinking before I went into the mood. I can't get the hang of it. I know when I get dark moods, but they descend so quickly and heavily, it's difficult to discern exactly what's going on.

The example I give Diane is a typical one, not a big one, just the kind of thing I might experience once or twice a month. I received an email on a Sunday night from a colleague, letting me know that a new tender was out for a big government account and we would be pitching for it. I read the email and froze. I lay in bed feeling sick, tearful and doomed.

I was terrified at the thought of coming up with new ideas for the pitch, as I was for every pitch. I was the most senior creative, what if I couldn't crack it? What if I failed to come up with the goods? I wouldn't be performing in the role I was appointed to do and they would all see I was a fraud. Other people would have to do my job for me, which would prove that I was crap. As for the pitch itself. All those people on the panel, judging me, thinking I was inarticulate and stupid. And the MD, watching me, thinking I'd never be the creative lead he needed. We'd lose because of me and we'd have wasted all that money on pitching. It was too much, I hated this job, I hated the choices I'd made, but I was dogged by the fear and threat of poverty. I wanted to run away, but I couldn't, because we had Farha and the house and I was trapped.

The mood got deeper and darker as the pitch got closer. I dragged myself into work, feeling like I was going to prison. I couldn't get out of bed and Farha fretted she'd be late for school. I thought people were sneering at me, I interpreted everyone's words as critical and threatening, and was ratty with colleagues. I didn't tell Dave how I felt – I didn't want to keep taking him on the rollercoaster with me. So I'd get quieter and do the scrabbly face thing, and he'd ask if something was wrong and I'd say, just a bit tired.

I stopped seeing friends and grew afraid of Facebook. I avoided neighbours and hurried into the house from the car, and vice versa. The housework was neglected (although Farha was always washed, with clean clothes) and my knees were so watery, I had to lie on the floor while Farha played in the bath. I did my finances over and over, wondering if I could do something else with my life, but I couldn't, I was stuck, I was exhausted, and sometimes, just sometimes, that little voice I used to hear, the one I had heard in the giant hall suggested the same escape. Death was the way out.

'What did you think immediately before you started to feel that way?' Diane asks.

I try to remember. Diane waits. And waits. My fingers scrabble round my jaw. I look at the clock. Forty minutes to go and the second hand is gliding round slowly. I don't know how to distinguish between thoughts and feelings. This is more than I can handle. I usually like a bit of nuance, but this is beyond me.

Wait a minute. Wait. I think I've got it. God, it was a fast thought though – so fast, I barely even noticed it happening. As soon as I read the email from my colleague, I thought...

Diane is so patient. She waited until thicko here fought through her brain sludge to get it. She looks at me with her bright, kind eyes.

'I thought,' I say, 'that I can't do this.'

'And?'

Shit, that isn't what she's looking for.

'And... I'd let them all down?' I say.

'And?'

Christ. What else? I think back. This is all I have, so I pitch it: 'That I'm not good enough–'

'Mmm. Remember I asked you to write down a list? Let's go back to that list.'

I flick back in my notebook to the page where, as part of another week's homework, I had to write a list of the things I felt I'd done well: two novels – one published, the other to be published in the new year – a list of account wins, promotions, awards.

'*Those* are the facts, Tara,' Diane says. 'Your work history and your writing success prove you are good enough. The way you're thinking is not based on facts. It's based on a core belief you hold about yourself. So what is that core belief?'

I look at her. I really don't know. I'm so stupid.

'It's what you thought when you received your colleague's email.'

I look at her blankly. I am daft.

'You thought "I'm not good enough".' She nods at my notebook. 'Where is the evidence that you're not good enough?'

I look at the list on the page.

'If there is evidence to support a belief, then it's a fact,' Diane says. 'If there's no evidence to support it, then it's just a belief. Your thinking is based on a belief that you're not good enough, but that belief is flawed. It isn't true. You can see that, can't you?'

What about the £20 bottle of champagne my old boss gave me for winning a major account?

She counters with the fact that my work did actually win the account for the agency.

I tell her about writing the first book and how awful it was and how long it took to get a deal for the second one and how I'm not as good as other writers.

'You've written two books and you've got two publishing deals. Those are the facts, Tara.'

I nod, fingers over jaw, thumbnail on mouth. Yes, the first book was a tough experience, but it was published. And it might have taken a long time to get a deal for the second novel, but I got one eventually.

Facts. I did with my life what I did in advertising: I took the facts and then recreated them, turning them into whatever would have the biggest impact. On me.

I explain how bad I felt when Farha was a baby and she asks how Farha is now.

Farha is six and made of starshine and diamonds. Whether she's eating beans, blowing raspberries or putting on shoes, I stand in her wake transfixed.

'Magical,' I say. 'Glorious. Sparkling.'

'She sounds like a lovely child,' Diane says.

'It's in her nature. We've been very lucky.'

'Tara, it's also how you and Dave brought her up.'

This is a revelation. A big fucking deal. I am shocked. Why not accept facts as facts?

'Let me show you something.' Diane gets up and goes to the whiteboard. She takes a blue pen and writes the word 'Thoughts' at the top of the board. Under it, she writes 'I'm talentless, stupid, inarticulate'.

'Those are automatic thoughts which come from the core belief that you aren't good enough,' she says. 'You think like this without even realising. Those automatic thoughts lead you to feel like this.'

She swooshes an arrow down to the bottom right and writes 'Feelings'. And below that she writes, 'Anxious, fearful, threatened, trapped'.

'Because you feel anxious, you think there must be something to really feel anxious about,' she says, 'so you start to feel worse. You ruminate on your feelings. Then you become afraid that other people will find out how you feel or that you aren't "good enough". That's why you end up here.'

She swooshes an arrow over to the bottom left and writes, 'Behaviours'. Below that she writes, 'Withdrawal, isolation'.

'That's where depression lies,' she says.

I nod, scribbling down her diagram.

She uses another arrow to link Behaviours back up to Thoughts at the top, so the whole thing is circular and I can see that one thing affects another affects another: I believe I'm not good enough and I automatically think I'm crap, rubbish, stupid, etc. This sets off feelings which also reinforce my core belief.

Then I get stuck, making myself feel worse and worse until I induce a physical response, expressed through things like wobbly legs made of water and shutting myself off for fear of people finding out how crap, stupid and disgusting I truly am. These behaviours also reinforce the original belief that I'm not good enough. And on it goes, round and round.

I understand.

'No one sets out to treat you as badly as you treat yourself, you know,' Diane says.

I look down at my notebook. I don't have any proof that I'm stupid, talentless or inarticulate. It's all in my head. I made it up.

She sits down and crosses her legs. 'Core beliefs are usually established in childhood. It could be something that happened to you, or something that someone said or did, that made you believe you weren't good enough. We need to find out where that core belief comes from. Were there any negative experiences in your early life?'

I tell her about the family splitting up.

A productive and destructive force

It's almost dark when I go to see Diane now, but the place is still beautiful. The grounds and surrounding lands are restful and the trees creak and hush without their leaves. My padded winter coat makes me outrageously big in Diane's office, but my discomfort is always quickly forgotten. She is warm, sincere and incisive. Her no-nonsense view is refreshing and often makes me chuckle.

We've talked about the family break-up, the shock move to East Way and my mother's depression, and I can see how and where the belief that I wasn't good enough was formed, and that it's no longer relevant. It wasn't even true or relevant at the time. It was something I created through 'emotional reasoning', Diane tells me.

Everyone interprets and gives their own meaning to the experiences they have, but 'emotional reasoning' is when you do it based on what you feel, not on the truth. I felt unloved, therefore, I thought, I must be unlovable. The truth was my mother was ill, but I made a creative leap, like many other children and adults do. They imagine reality rather than see what's truly there, and as life goes on, they create ways to reinforce their vision. Perhaps that's why so many creative people suffer from depression; together, sensitivity and creativity form a productive and destructive force.

Diane and I talk about my experiences over the years and we identify other unhelpful thinking patterns I've been using to reinforce my core belief that I'm not good enough. She hands me a sheet of paper which describes every one of my 'unhelpful thinking habits' and I read through them. I am totally textbook: Catastrophising: I assumed the worst all the time, e.g. I assumed my writing was shit and pointless. Why was I doing it? I was deluded and totally talentless. But evidence disapproved this. People told me they enjoyed my writing and publishers invested in it. No matter how I felt about it, the evidence suggested it must be good.

Mindreading: I assigned thoughts to other people when I had no proof of what they were thinking. I beat myself up because I assumed my boss thought I was lying about being depressed, but I had no proof of what she thought. I gave myself an unnecessary mental beating, which made me feel worse.

All or nothing thinking: I thought in extremes and could not accept alternatives or other options. I tended to think that if I didn't have creative success every time I tried something, then I was utterly luckless/talentless/God had it in for me. I didn't have any evidence to prove that I was luckless, talentless or God had it in for me. And anyway, life is more nuanced than that. Nothing is really so black or white.

Overgeneralising: this is when I made negative assumptions about something based on one or two experiences of it. I assumed everyone in the estate where I grew up was a stinking bully or sociopath because I had encountered a handful of people who were these things. In reality, I knew plenty of people from the estate who were normal and nice. But I couldn't accept the truth.

Ignoring the positive: because I was convinced I was worthless, I twisted successes and good things so they had a negative impact on me. When my work won a major account for the ad agency, I was angry and upset that my bosses didn't thank me personally. To me, it meant they thought I was worthless. Not only was I mindreading, I completely ignored the fact that my work won a major account for the agency. *My* work. I wasn't worthless. I was actually very good at my job. That had real value, but at the time I couldn't see it.

I'd been telling myself horrible things for most of my life. Now I could see that none of them were true.

Driving home from my appointment with Diane, overtaken by thundering lorries in the dark and soothing my thinker with a dose of Classic FM, a thought bubbles to the surface.

The belief that I wasn't good enough created my fierce drive to constantly prove and improve myself, and that same drive took me from penniless kid in a housing estate to published author and advertising professional. But it also guaranteed my feelings of failure no matter what I did. And then the drive would kick in and I would pick myself up and try again, working harder and harder. And constantly feeling I was a failure. And so it went, up and down and on and on, without relief. My core belief was another productive, destructive force.

I might not be able to switch off the drive, but if I used the drive to get my head round CBT, maybe I could finally get on top of depression.

I set myself to work.

Is this the Road to Damascus?

CBT takes practice, but I put the effort in. I stay alert to my moods and use my notebook to explore them, just the way Denise has shown me. If I notice a sudden plummet in my mood, I describe the situation that happened immediately before it and pinpoint the thought that went through my head. Then I write down the 'evidence' that supports the thought. If there is no evidence to support what I thought or if the evidence is flimsy, it's not fact; I've made it up based on the old belief that I'm not good enough. Have I used one of the unhelpful thinking patterns to get there, such as over-generalising, mindreading or catastophising? With the perspective this exercise gives me, I re-focus and write down the facts of the situation.

Day after day, I use this 'formula' to examine and reassess exactly what's going on in my head and my life, and experience more realistic and balanced reactions. It's strangely effective and powerful. A typical example is a day the MD wants to make changes to radio commercials I've already recorded. This will require re-scripting, re-booking time in the recording studio and bringing the voiceover artist back into the studio, and it will have a big cost implication. It throws me into a tailspin of self-doubt, anger and despair. The MD thinks I'm an amateur. I clearly don't know what I'm doing. I've fucked this up because sooner or later, I always do. No matter how good I think I am, I will never be good enough. I will never progress. I hate my job. I have made a mess of my life.

I take myself into a quiet meeting room and open my notebook. I start with the heading 'Situation' and I describe what happened between the MD and me. My next heading is 'Mood' and I detail how lost and angry I feel. I'm glad I'm in this meeting room on my own; no one can see me so full of hate for myself, so breathlessly trapped inside my uselessness. Then I write down the thoughts that triggered the mood: I am crap, I am useless, I am not good enough, ditto ditto ditto.

I write another heading, 'Evidence to support thoughts', and here I write:

- I fucked up the scripts and the recording.
- I'm costing the agency money – the client won't pay for changes, they expect me to be a professional, to know what I'm doing.
- The MD will wonder what the hell he was doing making me Head of Creative Development.

Below this I write another heading, 'Evidence that does not support thoughts'. I doodle for a bit, then I write:

- I've been doing this job for fifteen years and haven't been sacked yet.
- I've won awards for my radio ads.

- Clients may request changes, but they have never questioned my abilities.
- I've worked my way up and have been promoted to this role.
- Others, including the MD, listen to me and often take my recommendations.
- The MD is a perfectionist – he'd amend everything that is set in front of him, even the cup of tea you bring him (two teabags, not one).

I re-read my notes and mull over the evidence. If the evidence suggests I'm good at my job, if the MD promoted me, and if he and others, normally accept my recommendations, can he really believe I'm crap? Isn't that 'mindreading'?

Because the MD is a perfectionist, are his changes *really* necessary? How much will his changes improve the radio ads? 100%? Or 10%? If the improvement is small, it's probably not worth the expense of re-recording them. What if, instead of accepting his amends, I go back and ask how much he feels the changes will improve the ads in terms of percentages? He likes percentages and he has listened to me in the past. Maybe he will listen again.

I go up to his office and say exactly that. And he accepts my argument. Wow. I don't need to change the radio ads, they are fine as they are. They're not perfect, but they're still good, still fit for purpose. I leave his office, feeling as though my eyebrows are scraping my hairline. I'm shocked and relieved in an almost physical sense.

Something nasty has been lifted away from me. I almost skip down the stairs. Using the CBT formula to reassess the situation has had an almost alchemical effect. I've gone from a state of loss and despair to feeling fine and dandy within the hour. WTF?

Another day, I receive an email at 6.22 am from an unpublished writer I don't really know, telling me he's been shortlisted for some high-profile short story award. I'm immediately angry and despairing. Everyone is making progress but me. Everyone has better luck than me. No one likes my work. My writing is weird and shit, no one gets it. I am doomed to failure and mediocrity. And this guy – this guy I barely know — is trying to hit a nerve. Why else email me at bizarre o'clock? He must be warped.

Farha and I get ready for school and work and I find myself losing patience with her. I snap and shout at a child who is made of starshine. I'm a terrible mother. I drop her off at school, almost in tears, and I take out my notebook as soon as I get on the train.

OK, let's think this through. I have Diane's voice in my head when I question myself. Let's look at the facts. Is 'everyone' making progress? Who is 'everyone'? Just this writer I don't really know. And I didn't even enter the awards, so I can't really be disappointed or jealous, can I? Maybe I should just be pleased for him and hope he gets over his insomnia. If this guy is 'lucky', he'd have won the lottery by now or inherited a gazillion pounds from a mysterious aunt or have friends and loved ones to email about his success, rather than me at, frankly, hopeless o'clock. And at the very least, he would be published. Anyway, as the saying goes, the harder you work, the luckier you get, and if there's one thing I know how to do, it's work.

Diane's voice continues in my head. No one likes my writing? Really? This from a woman whose first novel was picked up by the first publisher she sent it to? Who received a contract for her second novel from another publisher? Failure and mediocrity don't really stand, do they, Tara? I've made those bits up. They are not true. The facts say my anger and despair are groundless.

It's hard to accept the facts when they challenge such deeply ingrained beliefs, but once I do accept them – once I understand that I am good enough – the mood lifts. It's astonishing. I feel like I've stepped out of a dark room to join everyone else on a bright and busy street. I send the writer an email (at normal o'clock) congratulating him on his success and wishing him luck. I decide to apologise to Farha and explain that I wasn't angry at her, I was just in a silly mood, and remind her how marvellous she is.

And then, well... then, I forget about it. I move on. I don't beat myself up or wring my hands over my crapness. The CBT technique stops rumination dead. I go about my day as though no mood depth charge ever went off.

I keep practising the CBT formula until, gradually, I begin to recognise and accept facts without having to explore everything on paper. New neural pathways are built, old ones left untravelled. It lodges in my head at a deep level: I am good enough. I really, truly am good enough the way I am. I'm not perfect, but I'm not completely shit either. After a while, criticism doesn't bother me so much. I don't feel so threatened or insecure. I stop comparing my own performance to that of others and condemning myself for being so crap. Believing I'm as good as anyone else means I grow in confidence too. Dave and Farha notice my good mood and I can feel it myself. It's not a manic, rollercoaster kind of happiness. I just feel pleasantly OK.

This must be how it feels to be normal.

My God, it's amazing. Liberating.

CBT at work

'You owned that room,' the Media Director told me as we spilled through revolving glass doors onto the bustling street. We'd just pitched to get on the advertising roster for a large public sector organisation. We knew it had gone well. We were cohesive, tight, enthusiastic and knowledgeable. We hit all the marks. The MD approved and said we gave a good account of ourselves.

We didn't even make it onto the shortlist.

'You can't be responsible for every reaction of the panel,' Diane had advised me on one of our Thursday sessions. In the past, if a pitch wasn't successful, I would know it was my fault: my evident idiocy didn't inspire confidence in clients and no matter how great the rest of the team were, we lost because I was inarticulate and talentless. I let everybody down. But now, it was different.

We had a post-mortem at the agency and examined the facts. We created campaigns that were proven to get results, which our clients verified. We recruited great people and kept training them, which is good practice. Our recommendations were sound, our creative campaign was impressive, and everything was based on research and solid thinking. Everyone spoke clearly and confidently. So why weren't we successful?

Maybe they wanted an agency with less talent, we joked. Maybe they wanted an agency who wouldn't show them up in front of their bosses. We had a laugh about it. I didn't run away, hide or cringe in the corner, because I accepted the facts; the facts suggested we were a good agency. The facts suggested the problem wasn't us, it was them.

As the magnet on Diane's filing cabinet said:

'Therapy has taught me that it's all your fault.'

It's not over

I've had a few wobbly patches since doing CBT, including a major dip a few months after finishing the first draft of this book. But I recover more quickly than previously. I stayed on the Sertraline and when that no longer worked for me, I switched to Vensir XL. I tried to come off antidepressants, but as soon as I encountered a major family problem, depression returned like a giant sucking slug and I went back on them. I'm certainly not 'cured'. I'll always have a weakness, but between medication and CBT, it is much more manageable.

I'm a bit kinder to myself these days. I try to give myself a break. I know to be aware of sudden plummets in mood and to examine my thinking immediately. I know to look for the truth and find a more balanced perspective, which means a lot less ruminating. I still ruminate on occasion, but I don't get so bogged down by it.

I'm still working and writing, and I watch Farha grow and I hope, like every parent, that I'm doing the right things. She is outdoorsy, courageous and thoughtful, and I read to her right up until she was old enough to throw me out of her room. Sometimes I would throw in a few poems, just to prevent potential phobias. She lights up our days and it's not hard to see that stars lived and died to make her.

I constantly second-guess my own behaviour because Farha is sensitive, and I don't want her to misinterpret my actions. I want her to have a different kind of life to mine. I would prefer her not to be so crazily, destructively driven, but satisfied with who she is. She is a determined person; when she decides to do something, she will work hard to do it and get it right. So she has drive, I can see that, but she also has a quiet confidence that dispenses with any need for approval. She does her own thing and I love that. I hope that having a moody mummy has not damaged her, rather, that having a creative mother has been good for her. The only dream Dave and I hold for her is to be happy.

Dave and I are still together – we are probably fused together by now – and I rarely tell him when I'm feeling low because I know he will assume the worst, even when that's no longer the case. But when I am feeling rough, just hearing him on the phone is reassuring, even if we have nothing to say. I wrote in my journal years ago that his love is a rope just under the surface of the sea and when I'm out of my depth, he keeps me up. He still does.

I miss my mother. She never got to know Farha's name and I regret that. She never finished knitting that big soft white blanketty thing, but I don't really regret that. I would have loved to share CBT with her, but by the end, I think she was starting to understand the truth about herself. She was not the stupid girl her mother made her think she was. She was bright and funny and owed herself kinder treatment.

It takes effort to constantly look for thoughts that stem from the old core belief, but I know how damaging they can be, so I try to stay on top of them. I do the things a depressive person is supposed to do: I try to eat healthily, not drink too much, take time to chill, see friends and family, take exercise. Exercise won't cure depression, but it has been proven to help, and a high energy dance class with ridiculous steps and a fun, kind (and if you're lucky like me, sexy) instructor will give you something staring at your navel won't.

Fatigue and stress are triggers for me, so I know I'm likely to be vulnerable when life and work get very busy. At the same time, I will always have the drive to achieve and improve and things are likely to be busy, because I drive myself hard and tend to overcommit to make up for the times when I'm feeling low. I keep my notebook handy and I still use the formula, although I need it less and less. Where antidepressants have been the difference between drowning and floating, CBT has been learning to swim. I am grateful for that.

Spring

I stand to leave, and I can see the trees and bushes outside are hinting at green. The daffodils have been and gone. We're almost done.

Today Diane took me through the sheets I'd been ticking every two weeks throughout the six months of treatment. The ticks move backwards across the pages as I tick 'hardly ever' and 'never'. I can see for myself: I'm less anxious, less despairing, more confident, more hopeful.

'You should write about this,' Diane says, standing up.

'About what?'

'Your depression.'

I scoff. 'No one's going to want to read about m–.'

She gives me a look. A look that says, 'After all this time, after everything you've learned, after all the work, after everything we talked about...'

I laugh.

'I'd love to read it,' she says, and I believe her.

I pull away from Holywell, driving between the landscaped fields and rattling down the slip road onto the M2. The radio plays McAlmont and Butler's 1995 song, 'Yes' and I sing along, surprised at the coincidence, smiling at the sentimentality.

Yes, I do feel better.

Epilogue

The publisher has organised a launch in Waterstone's for my second novel *Poets Are Eaten as a Delicacy in Japan*. Eleven years have passed since the publication of my first novel.

It's early evening and I'm nervous. Not cringing with dread and anxiety. Just a bit apprehensive. I'm worried no one will come. Maybe I'll stutter or spit when I read. My fingertips leave circles of damp on the cover of my new book. The cover is bright yellow with black doodles and scrawly writing – the perfect balance of happy and dark. I love it.

Dave and Farha are here, then my sisters and brother arrive with their partners, then Dave's mum, Dave's friends, my friends, my agent, my workmates, other writers (there are even some poets and I'm not afraid). There are lots of people I know and some I don't. It's a decent turn out.

Damian from the Arts Council gets up to say a few words, by which I mean long sentences pertaining to many different things. Sometimes he is smiling, sometimes he is serious, and his praise makes me blush. I look down and notice I missed my knees when I shaved my legs.

Do I believe Damian's kind words?

I'd like to. But I don't. Not really.

But I do know I don't want to die tonight.

Acknowledgments

My deepest thanks go to my husband and soulmate Dave, for your constant love and belief, and for coming up with the brilliant title of this book. Thanks and love go to my greatest creation, my daughter Farha, for shining so brightly every day. Wherever you are, that's where you'll find my heart.

I owe a massive debt to my dear friend Susan Feldstein for believing in my writing before anyone else, and to my agent Paul Feldstein for never giving up on this book. Thank you both for your friendship, faith and patience, and for masterminding the first edition of *The Upside of Down*. You goooooood.

Thanks go to Damian Smyth for opening my eyes and supporting me over the years; to Aoife Walsh, for her wisdom and sensitivity during the editing process; to Karen Vaughan, for the inspired cover; and to Malachi O'Doherty for his valued advice at the outset.

I am indebted to Dr Tracy Cruikshanks of Whitehouse Medical Practice and Denise O'Neill of Antrim Hospital for helping me up and showing me the way.

And for putting up with me over the years, I thank my siblings Christine, Karen and Mark, and their families. You are all saints.

Printed in Great Britain
by Amazon